ROUTLEDGE LIBRARY EDITIONS: LIBRARY AND INFORMATION SCIENCE

Volume 98

TRAINING OF SCI-TECH LIBRARIANS & LIBRARY USERS

TRAINING OF SCI-TECH LIBRARIANS & LIBRARY USERS

Edited by
ELLIS MOUNT

LONDON AND NEW YORK

First published in 1981 by The Haworth Press, Inc.

This edition first published in 2020
by Routledge
2 Park Square, Milton Park, Abingdon, Oxon OX14 4RN

and by Routledge
52 Vanderbilt Avenue, New York, NY 10017

Routledge is an imprint of the Taylor & Francis Group, an informa business

© 1981 The Haworth Press, Inc.

All rights reserved. No part of this book may be reprinted or reproduced or utilised in any form or by any electronic, mechanical, or other means, now known or hereafter invented, including photocopying and recording, or in any information storage or retrieval system, without permission in writing from the publishers.

Trademark notice: Product or corporate names may be trademarks or registered trademarks, and are used only for identification and explanation without intent to infringe.

British Library Cataloguing in Publication Data
A catalogue record for this book is available from the British Library

ISBN: 978-0-367-34616-4 (Set)
ISBN: 978-0-429-34352-0 (Set) (ebk)
ISBN: 978-0-367-41720-8 (Volume 98) (hbk)
ISBN: 978-0-367-41726-0 (Volume 98) (pbk)
ISBN: 978-0-367-81594-3 (Volume 98) (ebk)

Publisher's Note
The publisher has gone to great lengths to ensure the quality of this reprint but points out that some imperfections in the original copies may be apparent.

Disclaimer
The publisher has made every effort to trace copyright holders and would welcome correspondence from those they have been unable to trace.

Training of
Sci-Tech Librarians
&
Library Users

Ellis Mount, Editor

Volume 1, Number 3, Spring 1981
Science & Technology Libraries

The Haworth Press
New York

Science & Technology Libraries is published quarterly in Fall, Winter, Spring, and Summer.

MANUSCRIPTS should be submitted in triplicate to Ellis Mount, DLS, School of Library Service, Columbia University, Butler Library, New York, NY 10027. All editorial inquiries should be directed to the Editor. Refer to the Instructions for Authors page (at the end of this issue) for additional manuscript submission requirements.

BUSINESS OFFICE. All subscription and advertising inquiries should be directed to The Haworth Press, 149 Fifth Avenue, New York, NY 10010.

SUBSCRIPTIONS are on an academic year, per volume basis only. Payment must be made in U.S. or Canadian funds only. $42.00. Foreign orders: $48.00. Postage and handling: U.S. orders, add $1.50; Canadian orders, add $5.00 U.S. currency or $5.50 Canadian currency; foreign orders, add $10.00.

CHANGE OF ADDRESS. Please notify the Subscription Department, The Haworth Press, 149 Fifth Avenue, New York, NY 10010 of address changes. Please allow six weeks for processing; include old and new addresses, including both zip codes.

Copyright ©1981 by The Haworth Press, Inc. All rights reserved. Copies of articles in this journal may be reproduced noncommercially for the purpose of educational or scientific advancement. Otherwise, no part of this work may be reproduced or utilized in any form or by any means, electronic or mechanical, including photocopying, microfilm, and recording, or by any information storage and retrieval system, without permission in writing from the publisher. Printed in the United States of America.

ISSN: 0194-262X

Application to mail at second-class postal rates pending at New York, NY and additional mailing offices.

POSTMASTER: Send address changes to The Haworth Press, 149 Fifth Avenue, New York, NY 10010.

Science & Technology Libraries

THEME OF THIS ISSUE

Training of Sci-Tech Librarians & Library Users

Volume 1
Number 3
Spring 1981

EDITORIAL	1
INTRODUCTION: Training of Sci-Tech Librarians and Library Users *James M. Matarazzo*	3
The Indiana University Chemical Information Specialist Program: Training the Library User and the Librarian *Gary Wiggins*	5
Courses for Special Librarianship Offered in A.L.A. Accredited Programs and Implications for the Education of Science/Technology Librarians *Constance M. Mellott*	13
Online User Training: A "Team" Approach *Katherine M. Markee*	21
Training of Users of Online Services: A Survey of the Literature *Glenn R. Lowry*	27

Trends in Industrial Information Resource Centers
    Ralph J. Coffman
    M. Hope Coffman
	41

English Language Trends in German Basic Science Journals:
A Potential Collection Tool   55
    Tony Stankus
    Rashelle Schlessinger
    Bernard S. Schlessinger

NEW REFERENCE WORKS IN SCIENCE & TECHNOLOGY   67
    Janice Bain, Editor

SCI-TECH ONLINE   69
    Ellen Nagle, Editor

EDITORIAL

Those involved in sci-tech libraries and information centers should have more than a casual interest in the theme of this issue—the training of sci-tech librarians and the users of their services. A description of the scope of the issue's coverage of this topic may be found in the introduction written by James M. Matarazzo, Associate Dean and Professor at the Simmons College Graduate School of Library and Information Science. Dean Matarazzo is well-known for his writings concerning sci-tech literature and library operations, among his many activities.

When suitable manuscripts are received on topics which should interest the readers of this journal and yet do not happen to match the theme of any issue planned at the time of the manuscript's receipt, selected papers may be added as space allows. This issue features an unsolicited paper on the changing nature of the quantity of English language material appearing in German science journals, submitted by Tony Stankus and his two co-authors. Readers are urged to submit their manuscripts for the editor's consideration. A prompt reply is promised regarding the publication of such papers.

Ellis Mount

INTRODUCTION: TRAINING OF SCI-TECH LIBRARIANS AND LIBRARY USERS

James M. Matarazzo

Those who teach in the subject area of the scientific and technical literature and the employers of science and engineering librarians frequently talk about the need to recruit, educate, and provide a field experience for future professionals. These discussions, while laudable, have not led to any systematic plan to meet the needs of employers for subject specialist librarians. This thematic issue of *Science & Technology Libraries* provides a fine beginning on a subject which deserves action by both library/information science educators and those in practice. Perhaps, this issue will provide the impetus by describing the activities of some of our peers.

Gary Wiggins's description of the Indiana University Chemical Information Specialist Program is significant for two reasons. First, it provides a useful model of instruction for future chemistry librarians as well as chemists who will use and create the literature. Second, and perhaps most important, is the description of the positive efforts of this program to reach out to chemistry majors and attract these subject specialists to become chemistry librarians. This latter activity is critical if the schools of library and information science are to meet the real needs in this area of graduate, professional education. It will, however, require the efforts of both those in practice acting as recruiters as well as the best efforts of those providing the programs of study.

Professor Constance Mellott updates our information of the number of accredited programs which offer instruction in the scientific and technical literature as well as special librarianship. Her paper certainly provides evidence that currently enrolled students have the option to learn more about these areas while enrolled in Master's programs.

Katherine M. Markee's explanation of the Purdue University online user training program provides us with yet another successful model which can be replicated or altered to suit local needs. The challenge of training new team members to provide online services and to provide direct instruction to the end-user is one topic that is certain to continue to be in our literature and under discussion.

All readers of this issue will be grateful to Glenn R. Lowry for his fine review of the literature on the subject of online user training. His conclusions, drawn ably from the materials discussed in the article, could become the basis for action.

Dr. Ralph J. Coffman's essay on the industrial resource center and his thoughts on the requirement for cooperation between the end-user of

James M. Matarazzo is Associate Dean and Professor at the Simmons College Graduate School of Library and Information Science, Boston, MA 02115.

information and the information-processing professional demonstrate just how exciting, intellectually challenging, and complex our field is. The integration of various kinds of information in a corporation and the effort to achieve this level of cooperation will require the information resource manager to be an educator of users, management, and staff.

These authors, and the others in this issue, have provided the reader with an overview of the current and future issues in the training of science and engineering librarians as well as instruction for users of these libraries. While reading this issue, concerns will likely become apparent. If library educators and library practitioners could see these concerns as *opportunities available for solution*, progress in the training of sci-tech librarians and of the users of these services/facilities would be greater in the next five years than in the past one hundred.

THE INDIANA UNIVERSITY CHEMICAL INFORMATION SPECIALIST PROGRAM: TRAINING THE LIBRARY USER AND THE LIBRARIAN

Gary Wiggins

ABSTRACT. A program of study leading to the Master of Library Science degree which allows specialization in chemical information science has been developed at Indiana University. Prerequisites and course requirements are presented, with particular emphasis on the three Chemistry Department courses which form the core of the program. Course content and teaching methodology for those courses are outlined. In addition, the role of the Chemistry Department's Chemical Information Center (CIC) is discussed.

Introduction

A recent editorial by Dr. Herman Skolnik states that chemical information science ". . . is without a bridge to academic chemistry departments."[1] The author points out that most people who call themselves chemical information scientists moved into the field after careers as chemists in the laboratory. Skolnik urges each academic chemistry department to offer a chemical information science course and to appoint a faculty member to teach and perform the kind of research and development that advances the art and science of the discipline. Chemists have long shown concern for the formal acquisition of the skills needed to move freely and comfortably through the huge mass of the chemical literature. A number of studies in the last several decades have attempted to answer the question "Who's teaching chemical literature courses these days?".[2] By and large, the answers have indicated that it is primarily chemists, not librarians, who do the teaching. However, the Indiana University Chemistry Department has a long history of chemical literature instruction by librarians.

Chemical Information Specialist Program

This tradition led in 1969 to the establishment of a joint program of the Chemistry Department and the Graduate Library School (now the School of Library and Information Science) which leads to the Master of Library Science degree with specialization in chemical information science. At that time, the Chemistry Department offered only two courses in chemical

---

Gary Wiggins (BA, MA, MLS, ABD) is Head of the Indiana University Chemistry Library and Director of the Chemical Information Center. He is active in the Special Libraries Association's Chemistry Division. His mailing address is: Chemistry Library, Chemistry Building Room 1, Indiana University, Bloomington, IN 47405.

information. The first, C400 "Chemical Documentation," is a one-semester–credit-hour course, which, long before 1969, had been required of all undergraduate chemistry majors who were candidates for the bachelor of science degree. The second course, initiated in that year, was numbered C401 and titled "Research in Chemical Documentation." The intent was to allow upper-level undergraduates majoring in chemistry and Library School master's degree students to work on individually supervised projects for one or two credit hours per semester. C401 could then be repeated until a maximum of five credits had been earned for the course.

The present School of Library and Information Science (SLIS) course requirements for the special MLS program are heavily oriented toward information science and special librarianship. Three information science courses as well as "Literature of Science and Technology," "Special Libraries and Information Centers," and four other SLIS courses are required for a total of 28 credits. The remainder of the 36 hours needed for the degree are directed by the Chemistry Department and must include C400, C401, and C402. C402 is now the course number for the research course. It was renumbered in 1979 to allow a new two semester-hour course to be inserted into the curriculum. That course, C401 "Chemical Information Storage and Retrieval Methods and Techniques," concentrates on computer applications to the handling of chemical information. Students who complete the sequence C400-C401 are now fully prepared to participate in any aspect of the research conducted in C402. All three courses carry Graduate School credit, which means that they could count toward a minor in many of the master's or PhD programs offered by Indiana University.

Although the chemical information specialist program has been in existence for over a decade, the number of graduates is comparatively small, totalling less than ten. This is due in part to the fact that no attempt was made in the 1970s to publicize the special degree. The only written record of it prior to this writing is a scant six lines in the SLIS *Bulletin*. However, with the expanded course of study, that situation is changing. The School of Library and Information Science has recently printed a brochure for the Master of Library Science-Information Specialist in Chemistry program, and other attempts are being made to expand awareness of this course of study.

Although the minimum requirement for certification is a 25-hour BA in chemistry, all graduates to date have possessed substantially more credits, with two PhDs among them. Those who completed the program have had no trouble in finding library work. Among the places our graduates are currently employed are Dow, Union Carbide, Nalco, Eli Lilly, Bell Laboratories, and other chemically related firms, and two adademic libraries.

However, most of the students who take the Chemistry Department courses are undergraduates who do so either to satisfy a degree requirement or as electives. Class enrollment in C400 has grown from 33 in the spring semester of 1976 to 67 in the fall 1980 semester. During that interval, a total of 516 students completed the course. It is offered each semester and occasionally in the eight-week summer session. The course content of C400 is slanted toward the traditional printed chemical literature. *Chemical Abstracts, Science Citation Index, Current Abstracts of Chemistry and Index Chemicus*, other abstracting and indexing services, review serials, current awareness services, collective works (handbooks, dictionaries, encyclopedias, data compilations), and tertiary sources are all covered in the first half of the course. A variety of guides to the chemical literature are kept on reserve in the Chemistry Library. The basic text for the course is Maizell's *How to find chemical information* (New York: Wiley, 1979), which most students have found to be quite good. In the second half of the course, the major areas of chemistry and their specialized reference tools are presented. Throughout the course the goal is to impart to the students a knowledge of the communication processes which underlie the creation of the chemical literature. It is important to give them a time-frame which illustrates where the various secondary reference materials fit with respect to the appearance of the current primary literature. They must know not only what a review serial is, but also when they should turn to a review and what information they could expect to glean from that type of source. A total of nine problem sets are required in the course, each designed to illustrate particular facets of the chemical literature.

Although most of the students who take C400 are juniors or seniors, it must be kept in mind that stereotyped images and fears of libraries and librarians are present in many of them. I emphasize the fear aspect because it is my belief that most undergraduates will approach *Chemical Abstracts* only if forced to do so. Reading and hearing *about* this complex chemical reference tool can remove some of the anxiety, but nothing can substitute for a successful attack on the formidable volumes! Even with the decline in foreign language ability among today's students, it is necessary for them to cope with certain foreign chemistry reference sets, notably *Beilsteins Handbuch der organischen Chemie*. Our approach in such cases is to integrate the use of foreign language dictionaries with "back-door" access to reference tools. The results have been reassuring to the students, nearly all of whom are impressed with the scope and depth of coverage of such tools.

Chemists are an independent lot when it comes to searching through their literature. Thus, it is our belief that we should equip the students who complete C400 with the skills needed to do a thorough manual search of the printed chemical literature and the knowledge of the techniques necessary to cope with much of the information explosion in this field. There is one area, however, which cannot be fairly treated merely as part of a one-semester-hour course. One lecture on computer-assisted techniques is presented in C400, but the bulk of the material on that topic is covered in the second course in the sequence, C401 "Chemical Information Storage and Retrieval Methods and Techniques." C401, in its present two-semester-hour format, has been offered only since the fall of 1979. The course is inextricably tied to the operations of the Chemistry Department's Chemical Information Center (CIC), so a thumbnail sketch of the CIC is given below.

Chemical Information Center (CIC)

The Chemical Information Center was created in 1973, originally to implement online searching of chemical databases and to assume the operation of the IU SDI service based on the *CA Condensates* computer tapes. (Since 1969 selective dissemination of information (SDI) had been offered by the IU Aerospace Research Applications Center.) Thus, the CIC has over eight years of experience as an information center which provides batch SDI service directly from *Chemical Abstracts* tapes, at present, the *CA Search* tapes. Students in the advanced courses have the opportunity both to develop SDI profiles and to apply the techniques of information science to the development of other products and services based on the tapes. The goals of the Chemical Information Center are:

—to maintain awareness of current research and developments in scientific information handling, especially in chemistry;
—to adapt and apply new techniques and services to the information needs of the IU Chemistry Department;
—to educate and train users of scientific information, as well as information specialists and search intermediaries;
—to aim for full cost recovery;
—to engage in research in scientific information handling.

An unwritten goal is to build a reputation as the best and most nearly comprehensive program in all aspects of education for chemical information science that is available in this country. Our unique approach offers the student an opportunity to work in a research center where practical training can be obtained in chemical information science while working on an appropriate degree.

As mentioned above, one of the basic requirements of C401 is that the students master the techniques of SDI profiling and learn the structure of the *CA Search* database. Approximately one-half of this course is taught by Miriam Bonham, the CIC information specialist who constructs profiles for internal customers at IU and performs online searching of SDC and Lockheed databases and the data banks of the NIH-EPA Chemical Information System. Thus, instruction on these topics is provided by an expert information specialist whose skills are constantly honed through day-to-day use of the various systems. The weighted term search programs employed for SDI at Indiana University have been described by Roberts et al.[3] With some modification to allow for access to the increased number of searchable fields on the new *CA Search* tapes, those programs are still in use today. We eventually reached the conclusion that students should not have carte blanche in selecting the topics for the SDI project. In ths past, the range of difficulty of profiles of their own selection has been from very simple to very complex. Consequently, we now guide the students toward topics chosen to elucidate the main aspects of the *CA Search* database. Once the students have demonstrated their mastery of the SDI concepts and of the database, they are given the option of working with practicing scientists to develop SDI profiles on their current research topics. In addition to such practical experience with the CIC's SDI service, we also teach about other possibilities for SDI and current awareness, among them options available from vendors of online bibliographic databases and standard interest profiles produced and marketed primarily by the creators of the databases.

The methodology and scope of instruction for online searching vary greatly in library schools. Lancaster and Smith make a distinction between education for online searching, which concentrates on concepts and principles, and training, which stresses specific short-term needs, such as the mechanics of operating a particular system.[4] They feel that library schools should emphasize concepts that are transferable among systems, whereas database vendors should cover the pratical techniques needed to successfully search their systems, and database producers should offer presentations on the structure and content of their products. Thus, education by their definition would be the main area of concern of library schools, with training left to the vendors and producers of databases. In fact, education and training are mixed in many library school programs, but the distinction is probably an important one to make. In our programs, we make no claim to turning out experienced online chemical database searchers.[5] However, both education and training are offered. Particularly now that good printed exercises are available for online searching of *Chemical Abstracts* and practice files of *CA* are accessible through the major vendors, it is relatively simple for any program to offer some training.[6] In addition to this type of online bibliographic searching, students also search online one of the components of the NIH-EPA Chemical Information System, the Cambridge Crystallographic Data Centre file, which is available in a local adaptation of the Cambridge search program. Since much of the application of online searching of nonbibliographic databases has been to problems associated with the toxicity of chemical substances, those systems receive the bulk of our attention in this section of C401. An area which is outside the scope of this course is computer-aided synthesis of chemical substances.

Instruction in the online areas is considerably facilitated by equipment purchased in 1978 through a U.S. Office of Education Library Training Institute grant. A Setchel-Carlson video-monitor, Digi-Log computer terminal plus 5-inch CRT, and a Texas Instruments portable terminal were obtained as part of the grant. The video-monitor allows demonstrations for groups of up to 25 people at a time. Examples of both SDC and Lockheed searches are performed by the CIC information specialist as part of C401. A graphics terminal is also available in the CIC to search nonbibliographic files.

The final segment of C401, structure coding, concentrates on Dyson and Wiswesser linear notation (WLN) systems, with an overview of other types of structure systems (fragment coding and connectivity table systems). Students learn how to decode WLN and to encode in that system to the extent that they use it to access the few printed reference tools which include WLN indexes.

Unfortunately, there is no textbook which is suitable for the topics covered in this course. A copy of the bibliography and supplemental reading list will be supplied on request.

C402, the research course, is the final course in our sequence. Since a student may elect to take C402 without taking C401, projects involving both manual and computer-assisted research are undertaken. We take an applied research approach in the course. Harold Borko stated in a presentation during the Research Committee session of the 1978 Special Libraries Association meeting that library and information science research should be aimed at increasing the accessibility of information. If an information problem is defined, and the proposed solution deals with the problem in a nontrivial way and results in significantly increased accessibility of the recorded information, then we consider that a valid research project. Thus, the production of KWIC indexes covering areas or topics that are difficult to access is a valid activity in this course. An ongoing project is the provision of the capability for our SDI users to receive their output in machine-readable form and to be able to search their files much as they would through the major vendors. Still others have worked on pathfinders and guides to certain areas of the collection. Since the CIC makes microforms, the students even have the opportunity to explore microform as a medium of communication for some of the output from their research projects. To some this may seem as if we are using our students as a form of "slave labor." However, every attempt is made to insure that the students are learning information science concepts and methods as part of the projects. To the extent that they take away skills that can be applied to their own information needs or will help them to cope with information problems of their employers, these projects are valid research exercises. The CIC is a relatively young institution and may someday delve into the kind of pure research that is at present supported by NSF's Division of Information Science and Technology. For the time being, however, we have more than enough to keep us occupied with the application of research to our needs!

In summary, the Indiana University Chemistry Department has taken the view that chemical information science is a valuable part of its curriculum. It is hoped that other chemistry departments or library schools will heed Skolnik's advice to provide an academic bridge to this very rewarding career.

REFERENCES

1. Skolnik, Herman. Chemical information science in academe. *Journal of Chemical Information and Computer Sciences*. 20(2): 2A; 1980 May.

2. See for example:
Jahoda, Gerald. University instruction in chemical literature. *Journal of Chemical Education*. 30(5): 245-246; 1953 May.
Martin, Dean F.; Robinson, Dennis E. Who's teaching chemical literature courses these days? *Journal of Chemical Documentation* 9(2): 95-99; 1969 May.
Malley, Ian; Petts, Judith; Smith, Roger M. Education in the use of libraries and information in chemistry—an annotated bibliography. (Available from Loughborough University of Technology, Loughborough LE 11 3TU, Leicestershire, U.K.).

3. Roberts, Anita B.; Hartwell, Ieva O.; Counts, Richard W.; Davila, Roberta A. Development of a computerized current awareness service using Chemical Abstracts Condensates. *Journal of Chemical Documentation*. 12(4): 221-223; 1972 November.

4. Lancaster, F. W.; Smith, Linda C. On-line systems in the communication process: projections. *Journal of the American Society for Information Science*. 31(3): 193-200; 1980 May.

5. A few notes have appeared in the *Journal of Chemical Education* on ways that online databases have been introduced to chemistry students:
Drum, Carol A.; Pope, Nolan F. On-line data bases in chemistry literature education. *Journal of Chemical Education* 56(9): 591-592; 1979 September.
Krueger, Geraldine L.; DesChene, Dorice. Introducing on-line information retrieval sys-

tems to the undergraduate and graduate student in chemistry. *Journal of Chemical Education* 57(6): 457; 1980 June.

6. See for example:

Chemical Abstracts Service. *CA Search for beginners; an introduction to on-line access to CA Search*. Columbus, Ohio: Chemical Abstracts Service; 1980. (Note that there are different versions of this manual depending on which system you want to access.)

COURSES FOR SPECIAL LIBRARIANSHIP OFFERED IN A.L.A. ACCREDITED PROGRAMS AND IMPLICATIONS FOR THE EDUCATION OF SCIENCE/TECHNOLOGY LIBRARIANS

Constance M. Mellott

ABSTRACT. A survey was made of the 68 library schools with A.L.A. accreditation to ascertain the extent and types of their courses in special librarianship, in specific types of special libraries, and in specific types of literature. From the survey results it was possible to make an analysis of the extent to which these courses would serve the needs of those interested in science/technology libraries. The role of field work was also investigated. Statistics are presented on the number and types of courses offered and the type of field work available for students concerned with sci-tech librarianship.

Introduction

An important part of the education for science/technology librarians has often depended on courses given outside of library schools, such as an undergraduate degree or a second master's degree in some area of science and technology. There have also been some specialized interdepartmental programs, such as the one at the University of Illinois in the late 1960s.[1]

Within the library school, an appropriate starting point for viewing the education available for science/technology librarianship might be the courses available for special librarianship in general. A study of courses in special libraries and special librarianship as given in library school bulletins in the summer of 1979 led to additional questions on the relationship of course descriptions to actual course content, the frequency of course offerings, and the kinds of faculty members teaching the courses.

Originally the interest was in courses in special librarianship or the special library, but it soon became obvious that a broader survey was required in order to include courses in subject areas supporting special librarianship, such as those on specific types of special libraries and librarianship (e.g., law librarianship, medical libraries) and specialized literature courses (e.g., literature of science). Some of this information was obtainable from library school bulletins; other data, such as the frequency of the offerings and kinds of faculty teaching the courses, were not. A questionnaire (Figure 1) was designed in an attempt to compile such information.

Constance M. Mellott (BS, MSLS, MA, PhD) is Assistant Professor, Kent State University, School of Library Science, Kent, OH 44242.

SURVEY OF COURSES OFFERED IN SPECIAL LIBRARIANSHIP

1. Do you offer a course in SPECIAL LIBRARIES or SPECIAL LIBRARIANSHIP?
   yes_____   no_____

2. If yes, how often is the course offered?
   every term_____   annually_____   biennially_____
   other (please explain)_____

3. Credit hours (please give number)_____ and check whether
   quarter_____   semester_____   trimester_____

4. What is the name of the course?_____

5. Is the emphasis of the course on:
   a. administration of the special library_____
   b. reference materials used in special libraries_____
   c. survey of various kinds of special libraries_____
   d. other (please specify)_____

6. The course is taught by (check those applicable):
   a. regular full-time faculty_____
   b. adjunct faculty_____
   c. outside specialist_____
   d. other (Please specify)_____

7. The following courses for SPECIFIC TYPES OF SPECIAL LIBRARIES or SPECIAL LIBRARIANSHIP (e.g., Art Libraries, Law Librarianship, etc.) are offered: (please list courses)

Course Title	Taught by (a,b,c, or d from #6)	How often offered (see #2)

8. The following courses for SPECIFIC TYPES OF LITERATURES (e.g., Legal Bibliography, Medical Literature, Literature of the Social Sciences, Etc.) are offered: (please list courses)

Course Title	Taught by (a,b,c, or d from #6	How often offered (see #2)

9. Comments_____

FIGURE 1

Methodology

Pretesting of the questionnaire was carried out on approximately 10% of the total population (library schools with American Library Association accredited programs). During the pretest period, no suggestions for changes or additions to the questionnaire were received, and questionnaires were mailed to the remaining schools with A.L.A. accredited programs in April

1980. A second mailing (in June) went to schools which had not so far responded. Sixty-six questionnaires (97%) were returned, and the 2 remaining schools were contacted by telephone to complete the survey.

Courses in Special Librarianship

Ripin and Kasman reported that over 80% of library schools with A.L.A. accredited programs had courses in special librarianship in the 1974-75 academic year.[2] Responses to the author's survey showed 58 schools (85%) offering special librarianship courses. Fifty-seven schools listed one course; one listed two. Table 1 displays the course credit practices of these schools.

One school (included in Table 1) titled its course "Technical Libraries" and noted in the comments section that the "course concentrates on scientific and technical libraries but allows for student interest in other types of special libraries." Another school, one not offering a regularly scheduled course, noted a provision in its "Topics Course" for offering "special libraries" were there sufficient demand for it. A second school without a special librarianship course commented that this was an area of concentration, including electives taken outside of the department and a field experience requirement.

Forty-one schools (71% of those with a special libraries/librarianship course) offered it annually. Seven schools offered such a course every term, two every other term, one every third semester, three twice a year, three biennially, and one "when feasible," adding that "in practice. . .[it] has not been offered for at least 5 years." In addition, one respondent checked "annually" but included a note that while the course was intended as an annual offering, this frequency had not been achieved and that the course was "rather iffy."

Faculty

Thirty-eight of the responses (66% of those from the 58 schools with special libraries/librarianship courses) reported use of regular full-time faculty; one additional response reported use of a regular half-time member to teach the course. Four schools used adjunct faculty, one a visiting lecturer, and one an outside specialist. Others reported various combinations: seven had regular full-time faculty members and outside specialists; four had regular full-time faculty and adjunct faculty; and one had regular full-time faculty, adjunct faculty, and outside specialist checked. The one remaining response checked adjunct faculty and outside specialist.

Whether, in fact, an adjunct faculty member also happened to be an outside specialist cannot be determined from the questionnaires. Further, there is no way to determine from the questionnaires, other than from added comments, whether any of the schools reporting more than one type of faculty were using team teaching methods or simply had different teachers for different sections of the course or for different terms when the course was offered, e.g., summer sessions.

Table 1: Credit Given for Special Libraries/Librarianship Courses

Credit	No. Schools	Credit	No. Schools
3 quarter hrs.	6	2 semester hrs.	2
4 quarter hrs.	4	3 semester hrs.	36
5 quarter hrs.	1	4 semester hrs.	2
2 trimester hrs.	2	not stated	2
3 trimester hrs.	3		

Content of Special Libraries Courses

Courses with the same title vary from school to school, and catalog descriptions are not always a reliable guide to course content or emphasis. Therefore, one question was concerned with the emphasis or emphases. Responses showed wide variations, but 46 (79% of those schools with special libraries/librarianship courses) had checked "administration of the special library," some in combination with other aspects.

Twenty-one (36%) had checked only "administration," and one had checked only "survey of various kinds of special libraries." Fourteen responses (24%) had "administration" and "survey" checked, and two others had checked those and also "reference materials used in special libraries." Six had checked "administration," "survey," and "other."

Ten questionnaires had only "other" checked but one noted that "administration," "reference materials," and "survey" were included and that "the basic approach is to ask a variety of special librarians to talk about 10 or 12 'set' topics as they apply to their libraries. Naturally emphasis varies." Another response had the comment that the emphasis would depend on the instructor since the course had not been offered recently.

Explanations given when "other" was checked included "and the method to develop a library from scratch"; "management of literature found in a special library such as vendor literature, notebooks, report literature"; "includes planning information services for corporations, government agencies, and other organizations"; "problems in special librarianship and practice in development of patterns of service to meet the needs of specialized user groups"; "all aspects of current practice"; "field experience in consulting, evaluation of special libraries, extensive field surveys, automation of [special libraries], specialized services (e.g., SDI, abstracting and indexing)"; and "services of special library/information service and identifying users and their information needs." Many of these do include aspects of administration.

Courses for Specific Types of Special Libraries

A number of courses were listed for specific types of special libraries (Table 2). This part of the questionnaire was open-ended and some respondents listed course titles omitted by others, even though similar titles were included in their schools' bulletins. Some schools had more than one course listed in a category. When only one respondent listed a course title, the course was omitted from the table.

Also listed were: Analysis and Automation of Library Operations, Audio-Visual Services in Libraries, Federal Library Administration, Indexing and Abstracting Services, Library Service to Business, Management of Information Agencies, Manuscript Collections, Library Services to Ethnic Communities, Library Services for the Handicapped, Newspaper and Mass Media Libraries, Slavic Libraries, and State Library Agencies. The majority of the courses in Table 2 and those included immediately above as specific types of special libraries/librarianship courses were taught by other than full-time faculty. A majority were listed as annual offerings.

Other courses, such as On-Line Retrieval, Systems Analysis and Library Automation, and Government Information Sources and Services were noted in the comments section of questionnaire. No courses relating to engineering or technical libraries or libraries in the physical sciences were listed in the response to this section.

Courses for Specific Types of Literature

This section of the questionnaire, also open-ended, produced a wide variety of responses. Table 3 includes only those types of literature for which 15 responses were tabulated.

Also listed were such courses as Fine Arts Literature, Literature of Performing Arts, Chinese Historiography and Bibliography, Afro-

Table 2: Courses for Specific Types of Special Libraries Reported by More than One School

Type	Number Report	Percentage
Archives	5	7
Art	5	7
Biomedical, Medical, and Health Sciences	42	61
Law	26	38
Map	3	4
Music	12	18
Rare books, Special Collections, and Historical Collections	8	12
Special Groups, Library Services to/for	2	3
Theology	2	3

Table 3: Courses Reported for Specific Types of Literature by Fifteen or More Schools

Type of Literature	Number Schools Reporting	(%)	Additional Schools (from Bulletins)	Total Number	(%)
Biomedical, Medical, Health Sciences	32	(47)		32	(47)
Business	18	(26)		18	(26)
Government Documents/ Publications	27	(40)	8	35	(51)
Humanities*	51	(75)	7	58	(85)
Legal Bibliography	33	(49)		33	(49)
Science/Technology	55	(81)	6	61	(90)
Social Sciences*	54	(79)	5	59	(87)

*Includes a combined course for humanities and social sciences reported by 4 schools.

American Bibliography, American Indian Bibliography, Special Literatures, Music Bibliography, Environmental Resources, and Environmental Information. The last two courses are offered at schools which also listed science literature courses.

Three other questionnaires listed more than one science/technology course; Ripin and Kasman found 12 schools with more than one such course.[3] The percentage of schools with science/technology literature courses (90%) is also below the 95% figure given in the same article. Still, more schools reported offering such courses than any other type of literature course.

Most of the courses in government documents and the literatures of the humanities, social sciences, and science/technology were taught by regular, full-time faculty and offered at least once a year. A comment on one questionnaire gave the information that one school had dropped type of literature and type of library courses in 1979.

Field Experience

The comment section of the questionnaire also drew attention to field work as part of education for special librarianship. Seven questionnaires had references to field experience and practica, although no specific question on the topic was included. The seven schools were contacted by telephone for additional information on field work as part of their curricula.

This is not a representative sample of all of the schools but does include information of interest.

Credit for field work varied: one school allowed a maximum of six semester hours, with two placements for three credit hours each and with 50 clock hours required per credit hour. Another school gave one or two trimester hours credit, with 60 clock hours required per credit hour. A third school required 90 clock hours for three semester hours credit; a fourth required 72 clock hours for three semester hours.

Two of the schools also had internships or traineeships; trainees and interns were usually paid while students doing field work usually were not. One school paid the library a small fee for supervising the student. Most reported that no money changed hands for field work.

One school required field work as a part of its special library course, but also had a three-semester-hour practicum as an elective. Of the school's special library students, about 75% do field work in science/technology libraries. Most of these students do not have undergraduate degrees in related subject areas.

The other six schools do not require field work, although one school strongly recommends it. That school has a maximum of about 15% taking field work with about a quarter of these in science/technology libraries.

A school which has about 75% of its special library students taking field work has only one *not* in a science/technology library despite the fact that the school has very few students with undergraduate science/technology backgrounds. The only school which reported having many students with undergraduate degrees in science/technology areas reported that about 60% were doing field work but had no figure readily available on the percentage in science/technology libraries.

Still another school had few students with undergraduate science/technology majors, but more than half of the special library students take field work; over a quarter of these do so in science/technology libraries. The same school also has students doing internships in such libraries. All seven schools reported having one or more students doing field work in science/technology libraries.

Summary

Some areas of special library education seem to be well developed in A.L.A. accredited programs, such as medical and health sciences librarianship and law librarianship, with type of library, type of literature, and other related courses. Science/technology librarianship, however, is not generally offered as a separate type of library course at present.

Courses available for students interested in science/technology librarianship within the library schools are often limited to special libraries/librarianship (in 83% of the programs) and science/technology literature (in 90% of the programs). Some programs include additional courses in science/technology literature (or the literature of a specific science or technology). The opportunity for supervised practical experience in a science/technology library is also possible in some programs.

REFERENCES

1. Lenfest, Donna D.; Goldhor, Herbert. Interdepartmental training program for science information specialists at the University of Illinois. *Journal of Education for Librarianship.* 12(2): 84-91; 1971 Fall.

2. Ripin, Arley L.; Kasman, Dorothy. Education for special librarianship: a survey of courses offered in accredited programs. *Special Libraries.* 67(11): 504-509; 1976 November (p. 504).

3. Ripin, Arley L.; Kasman, Dorothy. *Op. cit.* p. 508, Table 2.

ONLINE USER TRAINING: A "TEAM" APPROACH

Katherine M. Markee

ABSTRACT. The provision of computerized bibliographic retrieval service is available at numerous libraries and information centers within the United States and in many countries throughout the world. This service requires specialized training for the users and the providers of the service. The training team is comprised of the database producer, the database vendor, the search analyst, and the end-user. This paper describes the team approach in training users in the usage of online services at a land grant academic institution.

Information systems have changed in response to data management and access demands placed upon them from all types of organizations. Access to information systems by computer has led to easy access of information and the growth in use of information retrieval systems. The amount of information stored is large but manageable with modern electronic data processing equipment.

As Lancaster said, "an information retrieval system does not retrieve information, indeed, information is something quite intangible; it is not possible to see, hear, or feel it. Information then is something that changes a person's state of knowledge on a subject."[1] End-users understand what it is you are retrieving, and online systems allow you to locate it. The items retrieved are usually bibliographic citations rather than specific information.

Online services in libraries and information centers have resulted in the need for training both the end-user and the search analyst. However, these two team members are only one-half of the online search service team. Other members are the database producer and the database vendor. The provision of online information requires a continual flow of communication between and among team members. This communication flow improves the access to information.

Lancaster sees online user education as an ongoing process and the responsibility for teaching the use of online systems for the retrieval of information as resting with the universities, where potential users of information products can be instructed before they get out into the field and become full time practitioners.

Training is an item which should be included in an organization's online service budget. This budget item should include initial search analyst training as well as continued training to refine the skills of search analysts and keep them abreast of changes in the systems which make the databases available.

At the author's institution, end-user training has been part and parcel of the online search service. The training guidelines were developed prior to the initial online training of the search analyst, as part of the implementation of computerized literature searching. As with all training modules or outlines, modifications and changes have been made to reflect the end-users' needs.

Within organizations providing online searching, the search "team" normally consists of the search analyst and the end-user. The search analyst handles the end-user's training. The end-user is the person with an information need on whose behalf a computer search is done.

A dichotomy exists in online searching between the mediated search and the direct search. The mediated or delegated search is usually prepared by the search analyst. The direct search is prepared by the end-user who prepares and conducts the search unassisted. The performance of searching varies among institutions, and the purposes, goals, and objectives of the information service determine the performance and conduction of the information query. Search query interrogation requires specialized training by the person or persons handling the information request.

As Wanger says,

> the original ORBIT system of the middle 1960's was not designed for either an information intermediary or an end user. In the early 1970's, when we were using ORBIT in an experimental context with the National Library of Medicine, one of the clearly stated goals was to enable end users to use the system effectively.[2]

It appears today that system designs aim toward a sharing in the search process by all members of the team.

The performance of online searching at the author's institution has been the responsibility of the author. The training of the end-user has been done by the search analyst.

A search service is only useful if it is used. Acessibility and ease of use seem to be the most important factors that determine whether or not a particular information service is used. The search analyst has realized the need to make the user aware of the service and consequently has marketed the service through brochure mailings, word-of-mouth, staff orientation, and campus publications. Marketing has made the target groups aware of the service as well as motivated persons to use the service.

Generally the way in which the service is presented has a significant impact on utilization and adaptation by library patrons. The search analyst normally has been the individual within organizations involved in end-user training.

The search analyst needs to be skilled in the mechanics of the system. Two groups from whom online training has been received are the database producer and the database supplier. If there is a search service manager who does not actually conduct searches, that individual is part of the group to be trained by the search analyst. Many students at colleges and universities are being trained in computer technology, and this knowledge is an asset when an online search is requested.

End-users seem to fall into several categories based on their knowledge of online searching and the use for which individuals could make of the search service: (1) the first-time user who admits to knowing nothing about online searching and how it can provide the needed information; (2) a person who has attended a professional meeting, had an opportunity to see an online demonstration by database vendors and producers, but still knows very little about the process; (3) a person who heard a lecture by the search analyst which outlined the type of information that can be retrieved; (4) the repeat user who has requested online searches previously. Repeat users include new staff members who worked at other institutions already providing online services. The educator, researcher, and practitioner have different information needs, and the work environment determines the specific information need. Undergraduates request searches to help them with projects and term papers; graduate students request searches to review the literature in their area of research; faculty or staff request searches to assist them in their teaching and research areas and to support grant proposals.

The search analyst is unable to train users without the ability to understand the requestor's need. Along with this ability is the previous training received from the vendor and database supplier on all system features.

As a member of the search team, the search analyst has a responsibility to see that the end-product meets the specifications of the requestor. The search analyst must be effective in obtaining the requested information as well as exercise good interpersonal skills. In a paper presented at the ONLINE 1980 meeting in New York, Marcy Murphy reported that in the training of online search analysts, neither general knowledge of automated or computerized systems nor specific earlier experience with searching seemed to be particularly important criteria in the selection of academic and public libraries searchers; both factors were given considerably more weight by special librarians.[3]

It is not within the coverage of this paper to discuss selection, training, or quality control of search analysts or intermediaries. Suffice it to mention that the effectiveness and expertise of the searcher has an impact on the online information service. The cultivation of satisfied users will pave the way for the continued growth and success of the service. User satisfaction will be affected by the search output, a feeling toward the information service, and feelings toward the search analyst.

This satisfaction includes the training given to users of the online service. The training programs given at the author's institution are the following:

1. The one-to-one presearch dialogue between the requestor/end-user and the search analyst. The presearch formulation affects the cost and effectiveness of the search. The analyst's skills are important at this stage in the search process. A careful discussion is made of the topic—the need for the information and whether it is within the subject coverage of currently available databases. If out of scope for databases, suggestions for printed indexes and abstracts are made. Working out the search strategy as much as possible before going

online usually produces a cost saving. It is helpful for the end-user to be present during the search so that any modifications may be made in the search strategy prior to finalizing the search.
2. Class guest lectures were given to the user community about the Libraries' Computer-Based Information Service (CBIS). Audiovisuals such as filmstrips, slides, or transparencies are used in the lectures. Handouts include a sample online search, the brochure about the online service, a fact sheet "tips to prepare for an online search." The lecture covers information storage and retrieval, online terminology, costs, telecommunication, advantages and disadvantages of online retrieval. An online demonstration is given at the end with students supplying key words. Many of the lectures are repeat requests with different students in the class.
3. On-site training sessions by vendors or database suppliers are given. Librarians and end-users are participants, and the search analyst corrdinates the session.
4. Off-campus lectures are given to instruct users who request a search by mail or phone. It is important that they learn about the interactive process of information retrieval to formulate their search request within the limits of the system's capabilities.

The search analyst shares user needs with vendors and database suppliers by attending vendors' annual update meetings, talking to representatives of indexing and abstracting firms who visit the campus to talk to the reference librarians, membership on database users advisory committees. Local and regional online user groups provide an information-sharing forum for search analysts and database vendors and suppliers.

As the search analyst interacts daily with the end-user, it is important to continually interact with other "team" members—database suppliers and vendors. Online searching is not a science but an intellectual skill. To keep abreast of information sources an individual must read, listen, observe, and absorb the contents of journals, newsletters, monographs, etc.

The author performs searches across all subject areas and serves the entire user community. To meet specialized user needs, subject area searchers are available in five school libraries.

Human factors impact on information programs and services. This impact on the acceptance and utilization of an information system within an organization cannot be overemphasized. Time is an important element in a person's job and scarce for the researcher, educator, or student. Online retrieval of information provides a way to save time. This time-saving element is coupled with the continued need for information, and at the author's institution the end-user delegates the responsibility for online retrieval to the search analyst. End-user training provides the means for that member of the online team to handle an information request and become satisfied with the results as evidenced by the growth in usage of online service from 43 databases searched in 1975-1976 to 3,536 in 1979-1980, exclusive of demonstrations.

The end-users of an information service are the people upon whom the service is dependent for its viability and continuance. Communication between all individuals in the online process in necessary—the interactive process. For the end-user to get the requested information, communication flows in all directions: database supplier—database vendor—search analyst—end-user. User education and training is regarded as a need in the computerized information dissemination and utilization process. Today's challenge is making online services available to end-users and their training by the other team members.

REFERENCES

1. Lancaster, F. Wilfred. *Information retrieval systems; characteristics, testing and evaluations*; 2d ed. New York: Wiley; c. 1979: p. 12.
2. Wanger, Judith. Some comments on the training and retraining of librarians and users. *In*: Kent, Allen; Galvin, Thomas, eds. *The on-line revolution in libraries*. New York: Marcel Dekker; 1978: p. 236.
3. Murphy, Marcy. On-line service in some academic, public and special libraries. A state-of-the-art report. *OnLine Meeting*, New York City: 1980 March: p. 17.

TRAINING OF USERS OF ONLINE SERVICES: A SURVEY OF THE LITERATURE

Glenn R. Lowry

ABSTRACT. A survey of the literature on the training of users of online services is presented, covering the period 1976 through 1979. Sections of the search deal with the general problem, the promotion of online services, the education of professional intermediaries, and the training of end-users, followed by a consideration of future trends.

Introduction

The author became involved in the preparation or education of online searchers in 1979 when he began teaching a course in basic information retrieval to undergraduate students studying information and systems science at Stockton State College in New Jersey. Some students enrolled in the course were later to seek employment as software programmers or as search intermediaries. Others were to become active end-users of databases. The course included basics of information retrieval, search strategy formulation, and "hands-on" practice sessions.

As a consequence of the author's interest in this subject, he prepared the following literature search dealing with the preparation of online searchers, covering the literature from 1976 through 1979. The sections of the search cover the background of the general problem, specific issues, promotion of online services, education of professional intermediaries, and training of end-users, followed by a look at the future.

Background Information

The desirability of providing direct access to computerized information retrieval systems for information consumers has long been acknowledged by researchers and system designers. The vision of an unassisted user interacting independently with a "friendly" system and satisfying most, if not all, of his or her information needs has been compelling and persistent. It has also been elusive. Artandi[1, p. 81] noted in 1976 that actual operation of such systems was almost exclusively performed by professional intermediaries, the very people that online systems were supposed to replace. In 1978, Peters et al. noted that intermediaries continued to predominate.[2, p. 138] This condition was also noted by Marcus and Reintjes in 1979[3, p. 2] and was the central problem addressed by them in their research.

During the relatively brief period since 1976, the concern of the profession as reflected in the literature over who should interact with the system has perceptibly shifted direction. In a 1976 review article, Marron and Fife[4] also noted the failure of online systems to alleviate or to remove the need for an intermediary. They cited several research studies which sup-

---

Glenn R. Lowry (BA, MLS, PhD) is Lecturer in Information and Systems Sciences, Stockton State College, Pomona, NJ 08240.

ported the continuing need for intermediaries.[4, p. 184] They noted that end-users usually did not use online systems frequently enough to become proficient searchers and that, in 1976, the cost of live practice searching was too high to allow widespread development of search skills by end-users. After enumerating the roles of intermediaries, Williams[5] discussed the advantages of using them. These included minimizing the number of search personnel needed, distribution of search personnel costs over a wider base, centralizing negotiations for services, minimizing the number of contracts negotiated by an organization, and developing a single record system for the searching activity.[5, p. 185] She concluded that a combination of end-user and intermediary participation was likely to continue.

At that time, however, there were indications that the ideal of end-user oriented systems remained an important concern. Martin[6] mentioned several principles of system design and objectives that designers should bear in mind. He felt that online systems should supplement traditional media. A user-oriented system should facilitate various levels of problem-solving and should not penalize common human errors, such as misspelling. The system should make it easy for a person who has no interest in mastering the system to succeed while providing the experienced searcher with the ability to exercise control. The system should make it simple to shift from a detailed focus to an overview and should analyze errors so that searchers will not repeat them. Measures of search proficiency are needed, as is a mechanism for sharing user experiences. Rouse[7] suggested that command languages should have a restricted command set and that fast computer response and provision for the searcher to review previous results without losing his present profile was needed. Like Artandi,[1] Moghdam[8] suggested that computer-assisted instruction would help end-users. Egeland[9] suggested that training efforts shift from patrons to intermediaries, while Sewell and Bevan[10] suggested that end-users learn when they have need to in order to supply their own needs. Marron and Fife suggested that interface standardization would greatly assist end-users[4, pp. 189-190] and that end-users and intermediaries need different sorts of training. Clearly, the profession was not quite satisfied with the state of affairs in 1976.

In another 1976 review article, Harmon[11] discussed basic issues of education and training which apply to the use of online services. He distinguished between training, which was aimed at skills development, and education, which stressed the acquisition and understanding of a broad knowledge base.[11, p. 348] He noted the increased demand by users for tailored services and the expected parity of manual and online access to information expected to occur by 1980. The strong role played by intermediaries was reflected in articles by Davis,[12] who discussed the role of information analysts in helping users to refine their requirements; Horn,[13] who described the role of the information specialist in mapping information systems and helping others to stay current with system changes; and Debons,[14] who advocated the training of professional information counsellors who interface data and user problems through a process of diagnosis, prescription, and follow-up of user needs. On the other hand, Stern et al.[15] advocated the active promotion of information services to users. Harmon noted the emergence of user-oriented information specialists and called for training of users as well as professionals. He called for a synthesis of intellectual and vocational methods for information science education and noted an international trend toward integration of information procurement with all forms of activity. He delineated the emergence of the theme of educating end-users, suggesting that user education should stress information access as a component of most basic and continuing education. He concluded with a call for study of the means needed to train end-users. 1976, then, was a year in which emphasis seemed to be shifting somewhat from the exclusive training of intermediaries to concern with the training of end-users.

By 1978, we can see that these trends continued. McCarn[16] noted that online services were growing at a rate of 40% per year. He suggested three basic roles for intermediaries: (1) the intermediary performs the search alone after negotiating search requirements; (2) the intermediary and user collaborate at the terminal at the time of the search; or (3) the user has access to a terminal and conducts his or her own search, relying on the professional when needed.[16, pp. 98-99] A user must conduct between five and ten searches per month to maintain familiarity with the system. He noted that the menu approach to guiding end-users unassisted through a search had generally been a failure and that online systems had actually perpetuated the need for intermediaries. However, since many productive scientists and scholars, prime beneficiaries of online services, prefer to conduct their own literature searches, a way of facilitating user-conducted searches is clearly required in order to significantly expand the base of users. A multimedia approach to user training was suggested.[16, pp. 100-101]

The 1979 review article by Wanger[17] pointed up the lack of a coordinated approach to online training and education. While training efforts of online services and database producers play a major role, the magnitude of these efforts has not been assessed, is not reflected in professional literature, and is viewed primarily as a sales tool by those providing service. As perhaps 45% of informally trained searchers learned from user manuals, more emphasis on those tools is merited.[17, p. 227] She calls for study of end-user motivation, the development of end-user/computer software interfaces, and for identification of specific end-user types. While it is acknowledged that end-users who do not want to conduct their own searches must be provided for as well as those who do, a clear need is expressed for more development of online systems designed to aid end-users.[17, p. 233] In just four years, between 1976 and 1979, then, we may note a developing interest in the training of end-users in the profession at large.

Specific Problems and Issues

A number of problems and issues emerge as the task of educating and training online system users is approached. Several vehicles for training and education are discussed by Williams[18, p. 324] including university credit courses, short courses, workshops, seminars, continuing education programs, computer-assisted instruction, training packages, and technical papers. Which should be used? Which are appropriate for a particular type of user? Writing from France, Moreau[19] addressed a number of problems attendant upon the creation and operation of an online information service. Some of the problems are inherent in the existing structure of the industry. These include too many systems delivering the same services in the same manner, persistent belief by end-users in the invisible college, end-user satisfaction with present documentation methods and distrust of new ones.[19, p. 241] Other problems arise from the use of new techniques and include passive training left to the initiative of individuals who employ user manuals and trial-and-error to teach themselves. She also expressed some difficulty in employing skilled searchers.[19, p. 241] In addition to these problems, she felt that the public thinks that it cannot afford online services and notes that end-users can currently rely on themselves to provide only 5% of their own needs. She cites the problem of infrequency of use and points out that promoters of highly specialized databases will have to rely on end-users, will have to identify and train their market. Finally, the end-users simply may not wish to reveal their area of research to an intermediary.[19, p. 243] It appears, then, that there is a need for end-user involvement which is accompanied by a somewhat countervailing end-user reluctance to use online services.

While Kaula[20] and Borko[21] expressed agreement with Harmon's distinctions between education and training,[11, p. 347] Peters and Detlefson[2, p. 135] identified three phases of user training as follows:

1. *Confidence phase*—gaining confidence in one's ability to use system
2. *Insight phase*—gaining greater understanding of the system and its potentials
3. *Incorporation phase*—system use becomes a regular part of the user's life

Clearly, a single training approach is not responsive to the varying needs of users in different phases of training. While it is apparent that the trend is toward greater involvement of end-users, there is some uncertainty as to when full-scale involvement might be expected. MacGregor[22, p. 346] felt that intermediaries would continue to dominate online use for at least 10 years and Martin[23, p. 244] also felt that large-scale use of online systems by end-users is years away and suggested that current efforts be directed toward more effectively training professionals. On a related topic, Hock[24, p. 212] states that a vigorous promotional program is needed to introduce online services successfully.

There exists, then, no shortage of problems in educating and training users of online systems. There is a pressing need for coordinated, effective approaches to these tasks if a fuller measure of system use is to be realized. Some distinct areas of concern emerge from the literature. In the pages which follow, we will examine three areas which are crucial to the development of effective online user education and training: the promotion and demonstration of online services, the education of intermediaries, and the training of a broad base of end-users.

Promotion of Online Service

Online services must be promoted because the uninitiated are likely to be unaware of their existence. Badre et al.,[25] writing in 1974, felt that a majority of science educators were unaware of the services provided by information centers, a particularly distressing situation as the primary use made of information centers and information retrieval systems was for research support.[25, p. 124]

Atherton and Christian[26] felt that sustained, dynamic promotion of online services is essential to success in building a broad user base. Promotion is the first step in user education. They suggested that market research techniques would prove useful in identifying potential user groups. A pair of fundamental promotional strategies are available: widespread publicity which requires a good deal of planning and resources, or promotion to targeted groups which permits gradual phasing-in of services. Successful techniques for promotion include flyers, publicity releases, brochures, price lists, bulletin board announcements, posters, bookmarks, formal advertisements in newspapers and magazines, direct mail pieces, newsletters, and reminders enclosed with paychecks or invoices. A particularly successful approach is the production of thesis preparation booklets and grant handbooks or guidebooks which integrate online services into the research process. Potential users become aware of the availability of services at the time of need which Atherton and Christian[26, p. 97] and Ferguson[27, p. 20] agree is a particularly important time to affect user behavior. Word-of-mouth testimonials are important. Initial searches for new users must be successful to reinforce system value. Marketing and promotion efforts should avoid the taint of commercialism.

Ferguson[27] focuses on the marketing of services to end-users. He suggests the identification of homogeneous market groups and that special promotional literature be prepared for each group. Personalized letters to selected groups and high quality demonstrations help to convince potential users of the possible value of online services for them. When considering promotion of services, thought should be given to identification of the specific group to be targeted, to determining their special interests, and to the development of means to serve those interests.

Crane and Pilachowski[28] offered some specific suggestions for demonstrations of online services to potential users. The demonstration should begin with definition of basic terms, such as database, interactive, online and offline. Other demonstration topics should include enumeration of the advantages and disadvantages of online service, explanation of the processes of database production and telecommunication, search strategy, Boolean operators, and SDI services. Their article contains a helpful outline for preparing demonstrations.[28, p. 23] Other promotional techniques, suggested by Schmidt,[29] include placing the terminal in a prominent, visible place, conducting on-demand mini-searches during announced demonstration periods, and encouraging end-users to be present while searches are executed. Vickery and Batten[30] reported the development of a multimedia teaching package, called Mediatron, designed to serve a variety of user types. They report that use of the package throughout the University of London has resulted in increased demand for services.

Vigorous, professional promotion and demonstration of online services, then, are seen as necessary to broaden significantly the base of users beyond that of professionals. Sufficient experience has been gained and reported in the literature to provide a basis for the development of online promotional programs locally.

Education of Professional Intermediaries

While some form of education of professionals as online intermediaries is to be found in most schools of library and information science,[31] universal agreement about the proper purpose or amount of education to be included in the curriculum has not yet been reached. Mott and Anselmo[32] suggested that information science education must center on theory and on theory-in-use. Swanson[33] refined this by distinguishing professional from liberal education. Professional education is focused on preparation of individuals for a particular type of work, based on the development of a broad knowledge base and on indoctrination with particular principles. She observed that education and prevailing practice are the primary determinants of the values and behavior of new professionals. A detailed curriculum development outline was presented.[33, p. 153]

Mignon,[34] reporting the consensus of a meeting of information science educators, suggested performance standards and requirements for students specializing in online searching. While he suggested that all library students be exposed to the capabilities of online services, new professional intermediaries should demonstrate system-independent mastery of literature searching principles, should fully master one online system, should be able to successfully execute an online search for an end-user, and should possess the administrative skills necessary to create and operate an online search service. Saracevic[35] recommended that applicants to professional schools be required to meet subject knowledge prerequisites in such areas as statistics, mathematics, and computer science.

Beyond specific courses, a number of writers, exemplified by Caruso,[36] have noted the need for extensive practice in order to gain competence as a searcher. A combination of manuals, CAI trainers such as TRAINER,[36] IIDA,[37] PIRETS,[38] and LADB[39] and system-specific training courses have been developed to fill this need. Harter,[40] however, pointed out some of the drawbacks of developing in-house search systems, either as commercial system simulators or as interfaces to specific databases. These include the disparity between the large files of commercial systems and the considerably smaller files of locally developed systems and the fact that, while commercial systems continually modify their software, it is difficult for local systems to make similar modifications.

The personal side of life as an intermediary is illuminated by Standera[41] in an interesting article dealing with the causes of tension affecting intermediaries. After chronologically describing the activities performed by a searcher, two high-tension activity clusters were identified. The first of these includes query-negotiation, system and database selection, and search strategy formulation. The second cluster includes the evaluation of interim results, the interception of errors, and strategy modifications. Some suggestions for reducing intermediary tension include providing greater capability for full-text searching, increased use of word proximity connectors, and standardization of command languages, record formats and file structures. Another approach may be to share experiences with colleagues, perhaps as a member of an online users' group, as reported by Berger.[42]

As professional level intermediary training moves toward standards of education and performance, as more automated practice aids and system simulators are developed to provide more economically a basis for significant skills acquisition and practice by students in professional schools, more activity is likely to be devoted to the ongoing education of professionals, as evidenced by a proliferation of online user groups and newsletters. As end-users become more involved in conducting their own searches, the role of the intermediary is likely to shift from that of all-important gatekeeper and general practitioner to that of consultant on more difficult, demanding information access problems. This will clearly call for high standards of training and background such as those suggested by Saracevic and Mignon. Greater professional skill is likely to be required by a body of informed lay journeymen.

Training of End-Users

Identifying the End-User

By the end of the seventies, considerable emphasis on the end-user began to appear. Noting that end-users had been viewed imprecisely as interchangeable units, Cole[43] suggested that refinement of the conceptualization of the "information client" was needed. Meadow[37] identified some important characteristics of end-users who are likely to benefit from online services. These include involvement in science and technology, familiarity with computers, reliance on sources other than libraries for information, and need for only a few searches per year, not enough to permit training to make a lasting impression. Caruso[44] felt that end-users were more difficult to train than professionals because they generally have no intrinsic commitment to mastering the online system. They can always opt to continue use of manual sources or to rely on an intermediary. While intermediaries are skilled at eliciting statements of information need and translating them into system-compatible terms, the end-user is most familiar with his actual needs. While the bulk of training efforts centered on intermediaries who provide the greatest access to information retrieval systems, it was suggested that efforts shift to a combination of end-user search for routine items with recourse to professionals for more difficult matters. Four steps are suggested for developing end-user skills to a first level of competence as follows[44, p. 224]:

1. Learning to use system hardware.
2. Acquiring skill and confidence in a basic command language and the ability to read output.

3. Recognizing searchable fields, choosing a database, and knowing how to access it.
4. Attaining competence in the use of Boolean operators to broaden or narrow a search.

Caruso felt that an end-user can achieve satisfaction with an online system when he/she can independently search one or two major services and knows one or two personally relevant files in depth. Beyond this, end-users may progress to independent competence and will regularly use online services when they can use several systems and files. Such an end-user must be highly motivated and must see online systems as a great benefit to commit sufficient time and resources to gain mastery.

Jahoda and Bayer[45] provided some interesting contrasts of end-user types and characteristics. They found that users who use a wide range of information sources are more likely to use online services than those who rely on a few sources. Generally, academic users requested more exhaustive searches while industrial users more frequently requested searches for facts and procedures. Older industrial users submitted search requests by telephone and tended to be more concerned with retrospective searches while younger industrial users were more interested in current awareness and in learning new specialties. Older academic users submitted search requests in writing and had a high percentage of exhaustive searches while younger academic users had a higher percentage of requests for specific facts and were likely to participate in the search process. User familiarity with online systems was divided into an early phase, representing the first three months of use, and a later phase thereafter. Later industrial searches tended to include more synonyms and search logic formulations with search requests, while later academic users included more search constraints. Observations such as these will aid in developing differentiated profiles of user types.

Turning to end-user interaction with online systems, Knapp and Gavryck[46] report that users revealed no embarrassment about seeking help in order to use automated systems. In a 1979 article, Meadow[47] made the most compelling case yet for the anticipation of a high level of user involvement. He felt that end-user training will become more common, significantly increasing the user base. Educated end-users can cooperate more effectively with professional intermediaries and will reduce professional time devoted to routine matters. Through an analogy with the proliferation of computer use brought about by the development of high-level language, he argues that command languages are actually first-generation online programming languages, knowledge of which is presently concentrated in the hands of a relatively few specialists. End-users will begin to learn command languages and to perform their own searches. This will create a demand for highly skilled professional intermediaries to conduct important searches. Higher order specialists will command higher salaries, increasing economic pressure on end-users to perform their own searches. The reference interview will be conducted at a higher plane than at present. Training or reference librarians will include skill in the assessment of the level of knowledge of search systems and databases possessed by the end-user. Thus, end-users will come to perform their own routine searches, relying on professionals for high-order consultation, spreading the base of online users considerably beyond the present level.

Training Approaches

While much of the literature of traditional library use training offers insight of value for the training of online searchers, the need for practice with a live interactive system, crucial to the development of online skills, imposes special demands. Writing primarily about traditional library use instruction methods, Stevenson[48] acknowledges the value of CAI as an online training technique. The most active areas of present interest in online training are those of user interface development and CAI. A brief review of several recent articles indicates that substantial progress is being made in this area.

Fairly early on, Goldstein and Ford[49] identified a key barrier to end-user searching in the necessity for a variety of end-users to optimize a single interface. While education generally recognizes differences in end-user classes, many software interfaces do not. The development of a variety of interfaces to serve different classes is suggested. In 1979, Meadow[37] published an article describing the development at Drexel University of a user-cordial system designed to accommodate most kinds of users. The system, named Individualized Instruction for Data Access, or IIDA, is intended to assist unschooled end-users. In a related article,[50] Meadow et al. indicated that IIDA is designed to diagnose user problems as they occur and to intervene with suggestions and tutorials when perceived problems reach a given threshold. IIDA has several modes, each with appropriate diagnostic criteria. The authors note that the interface is search service and database dependent. Meadow sees the end-user as a technical person who will need three to four searches per year, who is not an habitual library user. The objective of IIDA is to get end-users thinking in terms of planning of search strategies, to raise their consciousness of the need for an overall search pattern. The author stresses that IIDA and other end-user interfaces are not intended to eliminate the need for professional intermediaries. Instead, the intermediary's function will become more technical, more demanding intellectually. In an earlier article, Borgman and Trapani[38] discuss their experiences at the University of Pittsburgh with the locally developed PIRETS information retrieval system which was designed to permit novice users to conduct online searches without intermediaries. The system provides access to externally produced databases. End-users received a single two-hour class and a user manual. Class sizes varied between 2 and 20, and the authors suggested surveying class interests prior to beginning the class and varying the presentation accordingly. PIRETS guides new users through a "canned" search which provides a model for later search planning. Historical backgrounds and theoretical material not directly related to system use are minimized. Students had the greatest difficulty grasping Boolean operators and constructing search statements, as might be expected. Surprisingly, consultant hours were underused.

Simon and Doszkocs[39] reported the design of the Laboratory Animal Data Bank, LADB, which is an operational system designed to provide access to the data for scientists with no information retrieval training. It is designed for mixed numerical and textual retrieval. It provides command-oriented features desired by intermediaries while providing menus for end-users. At M.I.T., Marcus and Reintjes[3] reported experimental work directed at facilitating end-user searching through the development of a computer software interface. Work with six end-users determined that they were able to obtain a first relevant document, unassisted, in an average of 35 minutes. Results suggest great potential in the natural language based keyword/stem approach for inexperienced end-users. Niehoff et al.,[51] in agreement with the approach of Marcus and Reintjes, suggest that automatic subject switching from what the end-user enters to an authority term is technically possible, that it could be successful at rates between 59% and 95%. Ben David[52] reported the development of yet another software system which will permit an untrained end-user to successfully utilize an information retrieval system.

While Duncan[53] noted in 1978 that few training programs were aimed at special audiences and was less than optimistic about the likelihood of developing enough consensus for system standardization or for facilitating the transfer of search strategies from one database to another, she expressed the need for training of end-users in order to increase the online user base. Martin[54] was not optimistic about the feasibility of training end-users in public libraries. He noted that, in a public library, users are usually not knowledgeable about online system use or the topic of their interest. Most need an intermediary. Because of budgetary constraints, end-users are unlikely to gain sufficient experience to become proficient searchers. He concludes that end-users in public libraries are likely to receive online training only after all of the staff librarians have mastered searching skills.

At present, then, it appears that work directed at the development of end-user-oriented software interfaces is well advanced and that end-user searching through such systems is technically feasible. While some progress has been made toward generally identifying likely end-users to train, more work is needed to identify specific classes of end-users and to tailor software interfaces and CAI packages especially for them. Looking ahead, it seems that the next major groups of users to be trained for online system use are scientific, technical, and academic personnel. The final step in user training, that of bringing online systems directly to the general public, still lies in the more distant future.

Conclusions

While the issue between end-user and intermediary searching is far from settled, the existence of the technical means for an end-user to retrieve successfully information from an online system makes philosophical and financial considerations more pressing. The choice may become one of preference, as suggested by Brown[55] who works in an area where the researcher may not want to divulge current research interests to an intermediary. As the same documents are available in a given database for discovery by either an intermediary or by an end-user, personal preference may come to play the deciding role. Soergel[56] reminds us that the job of information professionals is to improve the user's task performance, as contrasted with satisfying him. An unassisted end-user may be satisfied before a crucial document has been retrieved. He adds that we are responsible for making the user successful rather than happy and advocates joint end-user/intermediary effort. Anthony et al.[57] reported the successful integration of online system use into a general engineering curriculum. Shirey, Gupta, and Debons[58] predicted a decline in need for information professionals trained at the master's level between 1977 and 1982 with a sharp increase in information workers trained at the baccalaureate level during the same years. Could this partially result from a shift from intermediary to end-user conducted searches? Perhaps another alternative may be possible due to an increase in the number of computer scientists employed in libraries to program in-house computers which support other library functions. Could baccalaureate-level programmers take on primary responsibility for actually conducting searches formulated by master's level information scientists, as suggested in another article by the present writer?[59] Perhaps the relationship could be much the same as that which exists between a physician and a pharmacist, acting jointly in behalf of a patient.

We may conclude, then, that future online user training is likely to contain emphasis on promotion of services, the education of intermediaries, and the training of end-users. Future efforts should provide for more substantive training for intermediaries in subject areas, for perhaps two or more levels of training, beginning with a phase in which the intermediary achieves basic mastery of search and system skills and an advanced two-year program, as advocated by Mignon, Meadow, and Borko, during which the student refines his skills to an acceptable professional level. More refinement is needed to identify and address the needs of specific types of end-users in terms of both subject interest and motivation to become their own intermediaries. It may be useful to view users as falling into one of three classes:

—Casual: users who want and need an intermediary.
—Students/technicians: may conduct their own routine searches, need occasional, decreasing degree of help.
—Productive scholar/scientist: will normally desire to conduct own literature search.

The literature of education and training for online use suggests that substantial progress has been made toward refining our understanding and methods during the past few years and that we are moving ahead toward refinement of the user/intermediary relationship in the decade to come.

REFERENCES

1. Artandi, Susan. On-line information systems in perspective. *Journal of Chemical Information and Computer Sciences.* 16:80-81; 1976.
2. Peters, Paul Evan; Detlefson, Ellen Gay. Impact of on-line systems on the clientele. *In: The online revolution in libraries.* New York: Marcel Dekkor; 1978: p. 125-148.
3. Marcus, Richard S.; Reintjes, J. Francis. *Experiments and analysis on a computer interface to an information retrieval network.* Cambridge, MA: M.I.T.; 1979.
4. Marron, Beatrice; Fife, Dennis. Online systems - techniques and services. *Annual Review of Information Science and Technology.* 11:163-210; 1976.
5. Williams, Martha E. *The impact of machine-readable data bases on library and information services.* Urbana, IL: University of Illinois, Information Retrieval Research Lab; 1975.
6. Martin, Thomas H. Reflections upon the state-of-the-art in interactive information retrieval. *In: Informatics, Inc. Annual Symposium, 11th, Los Angeles, CA, 1974 March 27-29; Proceedings: Information systems and networks.* Westport, CT: Greenwood Press; 1975: p. 79-98.
7. Rouse, William B. Design of man-computer interfaces for on-line interactive systems. *Proceedings of the IEEE.* 63:847-849; 1975.
8. Moghdam, Dineh. User training for on-line information retrieval systems. *Journal of the American Society for Information Science.* 26:184-188; 1975.
9. Egeland, Janet. The importance of user education and training in a multi-data base online network. *Information Utilities: Proceedings of the 37th ASIS Annual Meeting.* 11:120-124; 1974.
10. Sewell, Winifred; Bevan, Alice. Nonmediated use of MEDLINE and TOXLINE by pathologists and pharmacists. *Information Revolution: Proceedings of the 38th ASIS Annual Meeting.* 12: Microfiche I-F9; 1975.
11. Harmon, Glynn. Information science education and training. *Annual Review of Information Science and Technology.* 11:348-380; 1976.
12. Davis, Gordon B. *Management information systems: conceptual foundations, structure, and development.* New York: McGraw-Hill; 1974.
13. Horn, Robert E. Information mapping. *Datamation.* 21:85-88; 1975.
14. Debons, Anthony. An educational program for the information counsellor. *Information Revolution: Proceedings of the 38th ASIS Annual Meeting.* 12:63-64; 1975.
15. Stern, Louis W.; Craig, Samuel C.; LaGreca, Anthony J.; Lazorick, Gerald J. Promotion of information services: an evaluation of alternative approaches. *Journal of the American Society for Information Science.* 24:171-179; 1973.
16. McCarn, Davis B. Online systems - techniques and services. *Annual Review of Information Science and Technology.* 13:87-124; 1978.
17. Wanger, Judith. Education and training for online systems. *Annual Review of Information Science and Technology.* 14:219-245; 1979.
18. Williams, Martha E. Education and training for on-line use of data-bases. *Journal of Library Automation.* 10:320-334; 1977.
19. Moreau, Magdeleine L. Problems and pitfalls in setting up and operating an online information service. *Online Review.* 2:237-244; 1978.
20. Kaula, P. N. Education, learning, and information science. *Herald of Library Science.* 17:194-200; 1978.
21. Borko, Harold. Teaching on-line retrieval systems at the University of California, Los Angeles. *Information Processing and Management.* 14:477-480; 1978.
22. MacGregor, Alan. Some trends in research and development in documentation. *Journal of Documentation.* 34:342-348; 1978.
23. Martin, Susan K. Training for the whole on-line revolution. *In: The on-line revolution in libraries.* New York: Marcel Dekker; 1978: p. 343-348.
24. Hock, Randolph E. Providing access to externally available bibliographic data bases in an academic library. *College & Research Libraries.* 36:208-215; 1975.
25. Badre, Albert N.; Hughes, Dorothy; Ting, T. C.; Zunde, Pranas. Science information transfer for learning. *Information Utilities; Proceedings of the 37th ASIS Annual Meeting.* 11:120-124; 1974.
26. Atherton, Pauline; Christian, Roger W. *Librarians and online services.* White Plains: Knowledge Industry Publications; 1977.
27. Ferguson, Douglas. Marketing online services in the university. *Online.* 1:15-23; 1977.
28. Crane, Nancy; Pilachowski, David M. Introducing online bibliographic service to its users: the online presentation. *Online.* 2:20-29; 1978.
29. Schmidt, Janet A. How to promote online services to the people who count the most . . . management . . . end users. *Online.* 1:32-38; 1977.

30. Vickery, A.; Batton, A. M. Development of multi-media teaching packages for user education in online retrieval systems. *Online Review.* 2:367-374; 1978.
31. Harter, Stephen P. Instruction provided by library schools in machine-readable bibliographic data bases. *Information Management in the 1980s: Proceedings of the 40th Annual Meeting of the American Society for Information Science.* 14: Microfiche 3-G10; 1977.
32. Mott, Thomas H.; Anselmo, Edith H. Tomorrow and beyond: future prospects for library information science education. *Catholic Library World.* 47:391-394; 1976.
33. Swanson, Rowena Weiss. Education for information science as a profession. *Journal of the American Society for Information Science.* 29:148-155; 1978.
34. Mignon, Edmond. Emerging perspectives on the teaching of online searching as a professional specialization. *The Information Age In Perspective: Proceedings of the ASIS Annual Meeting.* 15:226-228; 1978.
35. Saracevic, Tefko. An essay on the past and future (?) of information science education - II. *Information Processing and Management.* 15:291-301; 1979.
36. Caruso, Elaine; Griffiths, John. A trainer for online systems. *Online* 1:28-34; 1977.
37. Meadow, Charles T. The computer as a search intermediary. *Online.* 3:54-59; 1979.
38. Borgman, Christine; Trapani, Jean. Novice user training on PIRETS. *Information Revolution: Proceedings of the 38th ASIS Annual Meeting.* 12:149-150; 1975.
39. Simon, Richard C.; Doszkocs, Tamas E. Implementation of a user interface for a complex numerical/textual data base. *The Information Age In Perspective: Proceedings of the ASIS Annual Meeting.* 15:309-313; 1978.
40. Harter, Stephen P. An assessment of instruction provided by library schools in on-line searching. *Information Processing and Management.* 15:71-75; 1979.
41. Standera, O. R. Some thoughts on online systems: the searcher's part and plight. *The Information Age In Perspective: Proceedings of the ASIS Annual Meeting.* 15:322-325; 1978.
42. Berger, Mary C. Starting up an online user's group - a case history. *Online.* 1:32-37; 1977.
43. Cole, Elliot. Organizational characteristics of the users of information retrieval systems. *The Information Age In Perspective: Proceedings of the ASIS Annual Meeting.* 15:70-74; 1978.
44. Caruso, Elaine. Training and retraining of librarians and users. In: *The on-line revolution in libraries.* New York: Marcel Dekker; 1978: p. 207-228.
45. Jahoda, Gerald; Bayer, Alan E. Online searches: characteristics of users and uses in one academic and one industrial organization. *The Information Age In Perspective: Proceedings of the ASIS Annual Meeting.* 15:165-167; 1978.
46. Knapp, Sara D.; Gavryck, Jacquelyn A. Computer based reference service: a course taught by practitioners. *Online.* 2:65-76; 1978.
47. Meadow, Charles T. Online searching and computer programming: some behavioral similarities (or why end-users will eventually take over the terminal). *Online.* 3:49-52; 1979.
48. Stevenson, Malcolm. Progress in documentation: education of users of libraries and information services. *Journal of Documentation.* 33:53-78; 1977.
49. Goldstein, Charles M.; Ford, William H. The user-cordial interface. *Online Review.* 2:269-275; 1978.
50. Meadow, Charles T.; Tolliver, David E.; Edelman, Janet V. A technique for machine assistance to online searches. *The Information Age In Perspective: Proceedings of the ASIS Annual Meeting.* 15:222-225; 1978.
51. Niehoff, Robert; Kwasny, Stan; Wessells, Michael. Overcoming the database vocabulary barrier - a solution. *Online.* 1979; 3:43+.
52. Ben David, Abraham, S. QUANSY - a basis for an intelligent front-end. *Information Management In The 1980s: Proceedings of the 40th Annual Meeting of the American Society for Information Science.* 14:96; 1977.
53. Duncan, Elizabeth E. Who should be trained? In: *The on-line revolution in libraries.* New York: Marcel Dekker; 1978: p. 257-259.
54. Martin, Anthony A. Training and retaining of librarians and users: reaction. *In: The on-line revolution in libraries.* New York: Marcel Dekker; 1978: p. 249-256.
55. Brown, Carolyn P. On-line bibliographic retrieval systems use. *Special Libraries.* 68:155-160; 1977.
56. Soergel, Dagobert. Is user satisfaction a hobgoblin? *Journal of the American Society for Information Science.* 27:256-259; 1976.
57. Anthony, Arthur; Sivers, Robert; Weiser, Virginia; Hodina, Alfred. An online component in an interdisciplinary course on information resources for science and engineering students. *Online Review.* 2:337-344; 1978.
58. Shirey, Donald L.; Gupta, Anand B.; Debons, Anthony. The future market for professionals in information. *In: Information science: search for identity.* New York: Marcel Dekker; 1974: p. 347-367.

59. Lowry, Glenn R. Online document retrieval system education for undergraduates: rationale, content, and observations. *Online Review.* 4(4): 349-356; 1980.

TRENDS IN INDUSTRIAL INFORMATION RESOURCE CENTERS

Ralph J. Coffman
M. Hope Coffman

ABSTRACT. Information is an essential part of any corporation's resources. Only recently, however, has emphasis been placed on the integration of various kinds of information services offered in the corporate environment. A trend has emerged to view the variety of information processing technologies from a general systems perspective, termed "Information Resource Management (IRM)." A major concern of top management is to to educate users in information as a corporate resource.

Information Resources and the Corporation of the Future

Corporations have evolved over the past 20 years through various stages of information systems. Early in the 1960s electronic data processing (EDP) was the only method of approaching information processing apart from human intervention. Throughout the 60s emphasis was placed on central resources in which various large databases were instituted to monitor (from an operations research or optimization perspective) fiscal, financial, technical, and scientific data. In the 1970s, however, as hardware costs decreased and throughput capacity of computer systems increased, it became obvious that a large central database was not an optimal answer to all corporate information needs. Decentralized subsystems were developed to solve specific management problems. These subsystems, known collectively as management information systems (MIS), were usually the responsibility of data processing managers, not functional managers. MIS systems were usually isolated from the user, and applications were usually developed in a top-down approach with little regard for end-user input into the design of an application.

In the 1980s high technology corporations, especially those in the Fortune 500 category, have decentralized to such an extent that systems can no longer be managed and developed which do not involve end-users in the design phase. This has tremendous implications for educating the users of industrial information resources. No longer are users isolated from the design and implementation of computing applications, including office systems, management systems, and information/library systems. Information networks, advanced telecommunications, and a host of new information processing technologies have now invaded the corporate environment. The corporation of the future is here today in many respects, and the

Ralph J. Coffman is Manager, Corporate Information and Library Services, Digital Equipment Corporation, ML4-3/A20, 146 Main Street, Maynard, MA 01754. M. Hope Coffman is Manager, Technical Information Center, Charles Stark Draper Laboratory, 550 Technology Square, Cambridge, MA 02138.

task of the 1980s is to integrate information processing technologies in this environment.[1] The high technology corporation now relies on various computer output devices, computer-aided retrieval, facsimile transmission, electronic mail, word processing, teletex and videotex, and even store and forward voice transmission.

Furthermore, this model of information services requires an organizational synthesis of four disciplines (information/library science, computer science, operations management, and electronic publishing) matrixed with services provided. Information professionals will need expertise in more than one discipline. Employees will need familiarity with information-related issues so that the information process that is accomplished is both cost beneficial and is consistent with job needs and corporate goals and objectives.

IRM: What It Means for the User As Well As Top Management

Information resource management (IRM) is a way of looking at a key corporate resource so that some value can be restored to internal corporate information and intelligent use of external information can be made available to those with a need to know. Educating the user for information resources entails a staged process so that the user can perceive her/his role as both a provider (of information resources within the corporation) and as an owner (of these resources in increasingly decentralized corporate structures). The user can also be a provider of information in the sense of being the originating source for newsletters, project and product technical reports; sales, marketing, and manufacturing status reports; exception reports to higher management; technology assessments; competitive analyses; and technology transfer.

This scenario of decentralized information originators in an information resource management program requires that the providers thoroughly understand their role of ownership of information. Without this caveat the decentralized corporate world can become chaotic, fragmented, and dysfunctional. It can become chaotic from the point of who has responsibility to preserve and protect information. It can become fragmented in the sense that information may be lacking certain safeguards on its accuracy, on its relevancy, on its authenticity, and, above all, the way in which it relates to other pieces of similar data or information throughout the company. The user as owner must be aware of how the information he/she generates relates to the aggregate use of it within the corporate setting, and this is a global security concern for top management. Finally, information can become a source of dysfunctionality to an organization in the sense that if it is inaccurate or misleading, actions can be taken which have nonoptimal consequences for the corporation. Within the world of the corporate information transfer process, each employee must be urged to examine his or her role as both a provider and an owner of information, linking the various information resources throughout the matrixed organization in a coordinated process.

The second major element in educating the users of information resources within the corporation is the education of top management. Before employees can be urged to view their place within the information transfer process of a corporation, there must be commitment from top management that such activity is not only condoned but supported. This is a precondition for implementing an IRM program. It is up to the various information managers within a corporation to demonstrate to top management the fact that specific departments are not only both providers and owners of information, but also interlocking and interdependent. Without this awareness and commitment from top management, information services can be rendered expendable and dysfunctional with each information service unconcerned with the organizational and functional interdependencies of the data and information provided.[2] This leads not only to excessive human resources and nonoptimal expenditure of capital funds in incompatible information processing systems and technologies but also to poor control of quality, timeliness, and usefulness of information provided. Top management must be aware of the interlocking interdependencies of information services and be concerned to view the company as a coordinated information resource environment with better information control. In this perspective of a total integrated information environment in the corporation of the 1980s one can see that educating the user/provider/owner is a central theme of corporate well-being, and it relates directly to productivity, sales, marketing, and finance, but it has traditionally been less visible to top management.

Key Information Cycle Components: Connecting the Supply with the Problem

What are some of the key information life cycle components that, as users, as providers, and as owners, the various levels within a corporation must be concerned? Figure 1 gives a hardware view of the cycle. First of all there is a supply phase in which information centers and libraries must be concerned about the availability of information for a particular problem at hand—whether the information is to come from external sources, such as online databases, books, periodicals, conference proceedings, competitors' information, or technical reports for instance, or whether such information is to be had from internal sources, sources that may have an implicit responsibility for financial, production, or administrative information but whose authority for assuming full ownership may not have been delegated explicitly. Of the external supply phase much has been written on various techniques of promoting the use of such materials.[3] For instance, in the whole area of online databases many producers and intermediaries have developed audiovisual presentation packages designed for customers. All too frequently, however, these presentations are designed for the information professional and not really for the end-user, and in many cases, therefore, supplementary background is required which may have to be provided through an industrial information resource center whose expertise requires them to deal with specific external databases such as technical, legal, standards, and patents. In promoting the variety of information sources it is important to focus not on the particular products of specific vendors but on the nature of the sources of information and the medium by

A HARDWARE VIEW OF INFORMATION RESOURCE MANAGEMENT:
A SYSTEMS ORIENTED BASIS FOR EDUCATING THE USER

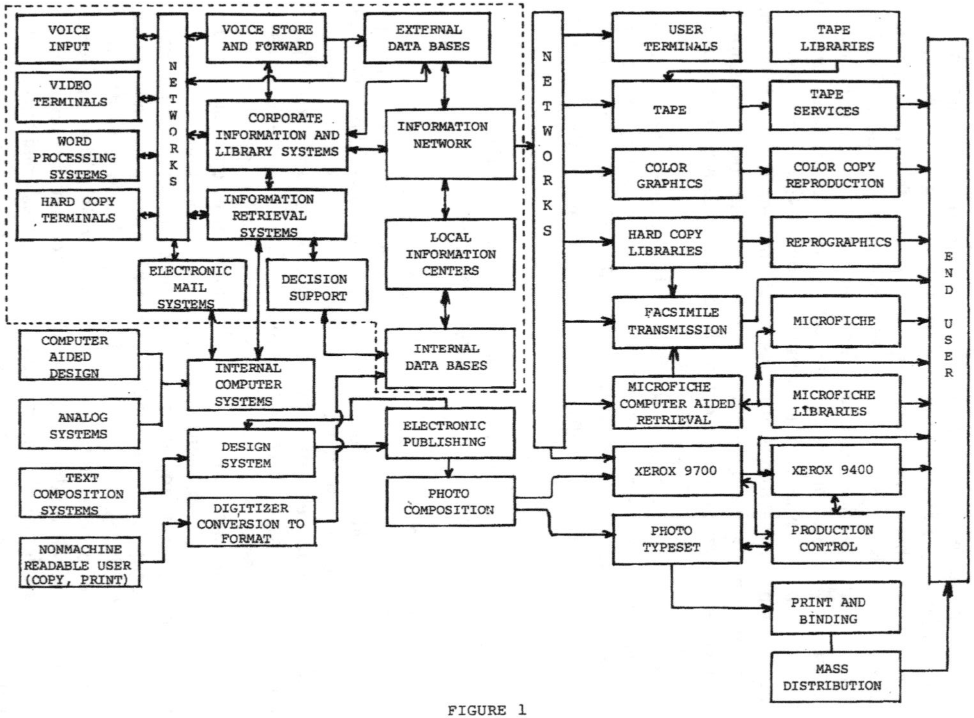

FIGURE 1

which it is communicated. In a survey of over 700 engineers (see Figure 2), communications media appear to be shifting only slightly in preference of electronic means. Still preferred are face-to-face or real-time telephone contact. It is this area of educating end-users to the benefits of electronic media that will be the chief area of advancement in the 1980s within Fortune 500 corporations. The chief issue is linking existing communications behavior as transparently as possible to user-friendly interfaces.

SOURCES OF INFORMATION USED:
A MEDIA RELATED BASIS FOR EDUCATING THE USER

Percentage of Engineers (N=732) Needing Information From Particular Sources Via Particular media

Local Colleagues	Nonlocal Colleagues	Internal Meetings	External Meetings	Project/Product Reports	Internal Technical Repts.	External Technical Repts.	Journals	Books	COMMUNICATION MEDIUM
87	12	69	21	71	07	17	--	--	Face to Face
43	28	04	02	08	13	--	--	--	Electronic Mail
92	67	12	--	27	12	--	--	57	Computer Conferencing and Internal Nets
09	04	--	03	--	--	03	01	41	Computer Conferencing and External Nets
01	0	--	29	--	--	12	--	--	Audio Tape
08	17	17	0	--	--	07	--	--	Video Tape
0	28	--	19	--	02	19	35	17	Abstracts (On-Line)
01	21	05	17	--	03	08	12	11	Bibliographies
--	57	37	15	71	39	37	44	32	Full Text (Hard Copy)
--	19	02	01	03	09	01	01	--	Full Text (On-Line)
18	29	34	02	21	03	08	--	--	Teleconferencing
0	17	--	02	31	03	03	03	02	Facsimile Transmission

SOURCES OF INFORMATION

FIGURE 2

Information service groups in a corporate environment do not sell information; they provide decision support and sometimes hard solutions to particular problems. When an individual wants to know of a special property of a particular alloy, for instance, the individual really requires numeric data and not a book, monograph, or periodical article on alloys. The information professional must be aware of the behavioristic communications patterns of an organization and be able to utilize internal networks and appropriate information processing that are consistent with these patterns.[4] The pharmaceutical and chemical industry has for many years been cognizant of the need of incorporating information professionals into the chemical environment employing information engineers postured to connect chemical engineering and research with information processing.

Other high technology industries including the computing industry have had less experience, on the whole, in developing specialized information professionals, partly due to the youth of some technologies. However, the trend is turning, with the net result that professionals are developing dual careers in technical as well as information processing areas. As information service groups find that they no longer are providing an information product or commodity but that they are providing decision support for a problem, many of the traditional aspects of the reference or research interview are going to be addressed by more highly skilled information professionals with technical, business, marketing, or sales backgrounds and specialized training in decision support.

Information and Human Resource Locators and the Corporate Memory

The changes in the role played by information specialists are a real factor in modern corporations. This becomes increasingly true when we focus on internal information sources which may be known only to very restricted groups, departments, geographical areas, or levels in an organization. Much of the initial work of educating users of industrial information resources is alerting them to the fact that the sharing of internally generated information can be a key benefit if reciprocated, but sharing also implies some loss of power and control.

It is incumbent on libraries and other information centers within corporations to take it upon themselves to provide and facilitate transfer of information about information. This is an area that on the whole has been not fully explored by researchers in information science or library science. To develop information and resource locator databases that are storehouses or pointers to corporate resources is one of the key focal points for the 1980s. Only through information transfer groups will corporations be able to improve productivity and provide the corporate memory to counteract decentralization and local autonomy which began to take over U.S. corporations in the early 1970s. In the information life cycle where internal sources of information and human resources remain hidden and obscure, it is the role of the corporate information and library services groups to provide coordination and facilitate guidance—a glue for the corporate memory.

Information Handling in the Corporation of the Future

The next point in the information life cycle is how information is handled. This involves a series of seven different phases each one with its own peculiarities, characteristics, constraints, and technical possibilities. The first, for instance, which we may label the collecting or source stage relates back to the user as an owner of information. There must be within the organization matrix management structures to monitor information processing so that outputs are consistent with end-user needs. The input/output model aligns with the sources of the information and the presentation of it to the end-user. (See Figure 1.) Between input and output several different components must be carefully designed, organized, and implemented, including methods of entry, transmission, storage, and backup.

Information may be provided in several media. For instance, we can think of the source of information as perhaps being a library with books or periodicals, or as a database that is generated by a manufacturing plant that indicates the throughput of that plant for each working day. The information in a manufacturing plant is entered usually by operators at consoles that are linked to central processing units and transmit information back to some corporate database for additional processing. This may or may not be sufficient. Usually this method of partial recovery prevents analysis of trends or noncurrent data. More formal information is stored in books or periodicals or corporate publications. Entry is no problem except for the fact that access points must be provided and, therefore, a catalog or information locator is developed. In this cataloging procedure the transmission phase to the end-user is an important one particularly as many corporate libraries or information centers are making use of sophisticated local, regional, and special networks for the transmission of bibliographic or locator data. So there is a problem in the library area of presenting secondary information, that is information about information, to relevant individuals and groups. Online systems that are user-friendly can help here and network access tools can be of assistance.[5] There is a storage problem that deals not only with the primary information being stored but also about backup and storage of secondary information. For library information centers, this is usually peformed by the bibliographic network involved. The storage of actual physical pieces of primary information, may involve various media such as books, periodicals, microfiche, microfilm, computer output microfilm, and video disks. The processing by which the primary or secondary information is retrieved and presented to the end-user may involve a variety of technologies, including distributed processing, text or image processing, electronic publishing, computer typesetting, spooling techniques, voice output, electronic mail, video tex, and teletex. Micro- or minicomputers may also be used to front-end large databases to do some intermediary processing for decision support systems, for instance, to provide specific answers to relatively restricted problems for particular internal applications.[7] The processing level, therefore, could take the form, for instance, of a library providing facsimile transmission of hard copy over telephone lines or through dedicated lines to other plants. The presumption here is that the primary data to be processed are not in machine-readable format and must, therefore, be converted to digital or analog format and then transmitted over predetermined communications lines to the appropriate destination where retrieval and final presentation to the user would take place.[8]

Educating the user for this complex information cycle, from the source to the final presentation, is a detailed and involved process. Adequate control of the owners and users is crucial if information in the corporate environment is to be managed properly. Users must be educated in the implications of their applications within the cycle of information resources.

The Information Audit

We have seen then that the supply, the handling, and the use of information all have dysfunctional implications if mismanaged. Users must be aware that they are involved whether explicitly or implicitly in information planning, organizational configuration, and communications patterns. Top management must be aware of the meta-data aspects of corporate global concerns such as systems development and control of records. Records management, forms management, and reports management are all merging in this new environment which must evaluate periodically the levels of information services provided, the organizational issues involved, and the human resource and capital plans committed. This information audit should be used not only in developing an information resource management program but also in gaining support of top management. An information audit can establish the climate for understanding information as a valuable corporate resource, and that responsibility and authority for information resource management policies and procedures can and should be assigned to specific groups. Information resource focal points should be developed for each organizational unit. Cost effectiveness should be a responsibility not only of the source but also of the user, a responsibility that can be promoted through resource sharing, coordination, and cost accounting for information services.

Corporate Information and Library Services: A Globally Oriented Information Source

A program of corporate-wide implications must involve the users as sources as well as users of information. Information proponents should be identified as to their roles as originators and as the sole competent sources of specific data or information. In this respect libraries as information centers are the sole competent sources of access to external databases, to books through national networking organizations, to library loans, to periodical articles, to a whole host of reference services that interlock with external and internal information suppliers. Libraries or industrial information resource centers are the most globally oriented sole competent source in any corporation. Other units within a corporation have information specialities, but it is the corporate information and library services component that has the widest purview of how information is being used both internally and externally. It is this group that is best qualified to provide the leadership, direction, and cohesion among other information processing and service groups throughout the corporation.

The Cost of Information: An Educational As Well As Financial Issue

A major concern in information services is the problem of developing and managing information handling budgets. This is of particular concern in a corporate environment where information services are unequally provided to various components of the organization—unequal in the sense that the amount and cost of information varies with the problems that users present to information resource handlers. That is, users as information proponents present varying degrees of complexity of problems to those sole competent sources that have been charged with responsibility by the corporation to distribute equitably the financial resources to the various information handling groups. Either central funding must be instituted to underwrite information services (with appropriate information audits and cost accounting structures) or chargeback schemes must be instituted in which users are assessed for the provision of information to them on a by-use or subscription basis. Some corporations combine the two approaches and operate with certain dollar minimums for chargebacks since charges against profit centers and cost centers within a Fortune 500 organization are relatively expensive, and, therefore, minimum levels of chargebacks ensure the fact that only significant costs are being transferred from one budget to another. In a survey of industrial information systems and academic research libraries (see Figure 3), a fundamental cost typology was identified.

Companies whose information services were not decentralized had an average cost per user between $7 and $9. Companies which were decentralized had a cost per user between $17 and $34. One organization which was primarily oriented to R&D had an average cost per user over $300. In this instance, the R&D organization did not correspond to the 80/20 rule (4 technical workers to 1 gatekeeper). Rather, each technical worker functioned as a gatekeeper, and this corporate R&D model corresponds to the academic research center. However, the cost per service transaction unit (STU) appeared to be the significant measurement of ROI. In this respect, academic research centers appear to be more efficient than most industrial information research centers. Only three Fortune 500 companies had an average cost per STU comparable (at $7.15, $25.40, and $31.48) to STU costs in American universities. Since two of these corporations were decentralized with 14 and 20 research centers and one with only four research centers, the issue of decentralization is not the determining factor in industrial information center efficiency. Rather, it is adequate education of end-users so that throughput of the centers makes a significant impact on the organization. Education of the end-user, therefore, is the single most important factor in providing services within the corporate setting. Industrial information processing centers in the IRM envi-

COMPARISON OF RESEARCH LIBRARIES' SERVICES:
A SERVICE ORIENTED BASIS FOR EDUCATING THE USER

FORTUNE 500 HIGH TECHNOLOGY CORPORATIONS

User Populations (000's)	# Libs.	Lib. Cost/User (to nearest $)	Employees/ Lib. Staff (000's)	Service Transaction Units (000's) Per Annum					Promotional Communications Implemented**
				Reference	Doc. Delivery	Online Searches	Total	Average Cost	
292	26	17.00	2.6	N.A.	N.A.	N.A.	N.A.	N.A.	1-9
106	5	9.00	5.3	.23	5.0	.12	5.35	170.09	1-6, 9
101	11	34.00	1.3	23.1	13.3	9.5	45.9	76.51	1-5, 8
98	13	15.00	3.0	--	13.0	1.5	14.5	103.79	1-3, 5, 9
92	22	20.00	2.1	--	12.0	2.0	14.0	131.28	1-3, 5-6, 9
79	4	7.00	7.1	2.1	18.0	.4	20.5	25.40	1-3, 5
51	4	8.00	5.7	N.A.	N.A.	N.A.	N.A.	N.A.	1-3, 6
45	3	9.00	5.0	--	7.0	--	7.0	60.71	1-10
44	14	18.00	2.7	63.1	46.4	1.8	111.3	7.15	1-9
17	20	312.00	.14	--	149.6	19.2	166.8	31.48	

AMERICAN UNIVERSITIES

45*	7	50.00	.26	28.8	62.7	.4	91.9	24.30	1-2, 4, 6-10
21	96	823.00	.03	181.2	1,956.7	2.7	2,140.6	8.08	1-2, 4-5
14	26	814.00	.03	24.2	802.3	.7	827.2	13.78	1-2, 4-6
10	14	348.00	.05	104.0	451.6	.8	556.4	6.25	1-2, 4-6
6	2	146.00	.11	2.6	123.5	.3	126.4	6.36	1-2, 4-6

* This column denotes full-time enrollment and full-time teaching staff.

** See figure 4 "Promotional Communications Implemented" for key listing the ten types.

FIGURE 3

ronment are committed to operate within a network in which each is a member of the corporate information structure acting as information brokers to the rest of the corporation.

Industrial information processing centers, therefore, behave very much like their commercial counterparts. Information presented to users must be justified financially to that user. A whole host of federal and local legislation is dealing with this area of making reasonable cost accounting structures operative in all domains of public and private life. The same mechanism operates within the corporate structure. Information services within a corporation provide resources much as a utility company provides resources to its customers. The level of service must be warranted by the nature of the need. Information managers must educate their customers in the complexities of developing such reasonable structures based on actual costs and throughput of services. Along with top management's consent to looking at the broad program, cutting across functional lines, it is equally important to have support from financial analysts for each of the information utilities provided within the organization to ensure cohesive and consistent policies of access to information resources. Very little in the external literature has been written from the point of view of financial analysts on this topic, but with the fast developing technologies being implemented in the larger corporations in the 1980s such responsibilities will increasingly dominate the attention of the financial personnel attached to information centers.

Information resource management tools must be provided to the users of scientific and technical information within a corporate setting that can help orient the community. Industrial information resource centers, through development of catalogs, indexing techniques, and classification schemes, have been intimately concerned with providing levels of access. However, in scientific and technical literature, bibliographic standards provide very little assistance for assessing rapidly evolving terminology.[9] Techniques today which can facilitate better access to data can involve various methods of automated indexing, sophisticated query languages for use with either bibliographic or full text databases, various stemming algorithms for application to natural language recall and development of data dictionaries or information resource directories providing pointers to large stores of information which are not themselves fully indexed or otherwise identifiable. Corporate information services must find ways in which the various standard bibliographic retrieval policies established either by the Library of Congress, or the Anglo-American Cataloging Rules, or the Universal Decimal Classification System, for example, can be supplemented or replaced by techniques which allow fast, specific, natural lanaguage retrieval. To a large extent commerical databases have filled the gap between natural language and standard subject approaches, but corporations are not mainly concerned with literature published in the external environment. High level query languages may provide the best way of dealing with proprietary types of data and information. Central to educating the corporate user of proprietary information is to indicate the ways in which various existing databases can be manipulated. The development of model prototype information retrieval systems can facilitate a crucial level of education for the end-user to begin to assess how feasible it is for technical literature to be accessible online to the technical and scientific groups. Communication processes hitherto studied behavioristically can be implemented by such models. In addition to seminars developed by professional schools, many database producers or intermediaries are providing their own training for online searching, as we have noted. Information professionals within a corporate organization are in an excellent position to be able to give demonstrations of various kinds of manipulation of online databases to their clientele, both the information professional and the sophisticated end-user.

A key element in the success of an information management program is to involve the information specialist directly with specific scientific and technical projects. Top management should be aware that the information specialists contribute to the productivity of the company through their being able to provide essential information which leads to development of the corporate products. Unnecessary redundancy of scientific and technical studies, and development of identical or similar projects need not occur if information specialists are involved at the appropriate time in project or product development.

Educational Programs

Education for IRM should be promoted to those who are in the decision-making process, the product development managers, and top management through appropriate vehicles for disseminating the ways in which an IRM program can visibly impact the organization (see Figure 4). Through personnel departments at hiring time, slide/tape or videotape presentations can be given new employees along with engineering and technical standards by which the scientific and technical community is expected to live. It is critical to educate the new employee through the personnel organization as to the availability of information resources within the corporation. In addition to generalized presentations of a formal nature, existing personnel should be updated through structured broadcasting about events taking place within their specific fields of endeavor and within the specific areas where they as information owners have a particular responsibility to the corporate community at large. Newletters, seminar series, and small planning councils clustered around selected technologies can be most beneficial in educating users in the effective access to information within the corporate setting in which disciplines, functions, and organizational structure are coordinated in harmony.

Educating users of industrial information resource centers requires a program of coordinated effort, especially for the Fortune 500 company. Education extends from the level of gaining top management support to the level of gaining user involvement in design and acceptance of the implementation. Above all it requires close coordination within all of the information processing functions to ensure a coherent plan. As we enter the 1980s the closer cooperation of end-user with information processing professionals may provide the environment for a truly dynamic corporate information resource management era.

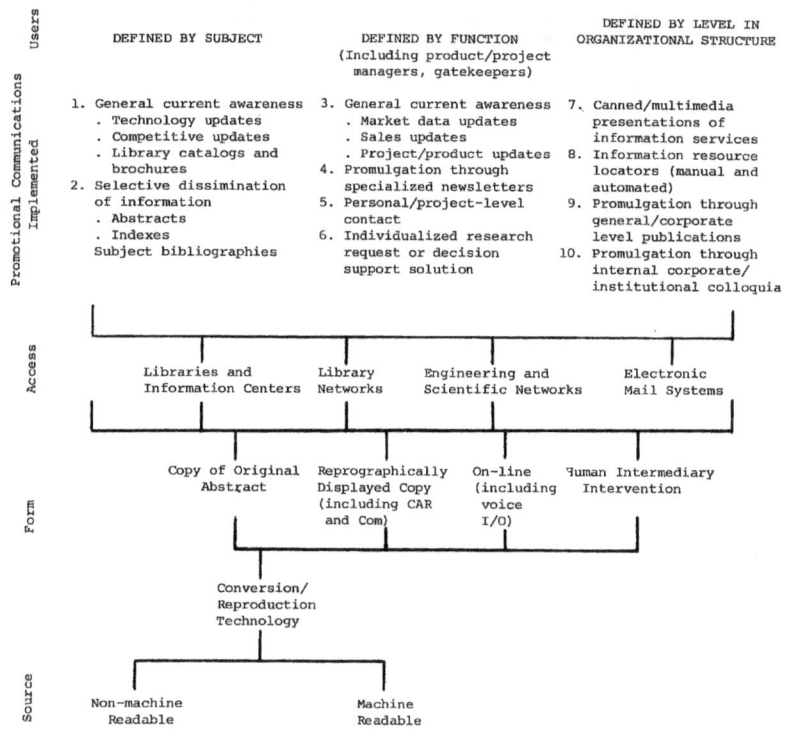

FIGURE 4

REFERENCES

1. Uhlig, Ronald P.; Farber, David J.; Bair, James H. *The office of the future: communication and computers*. Amsterdam: North Holland Publishing Co.; 1979: p. 111-122. (Monograph Series of the International Council for Computer Communications)
2. Lawler, Edward E. III; Rhode, John Grant. *Information and control in organizations*. Santa Monica, CA.: Goodyear Publishing Co.; 1976: p. 150-152.
3. Caruso, Elaine. Hands on online: bringing it home. *Online Review*. 2(3): 251-268; 1978.
4. Allen, Thomas J. *Managing the flow of technology*. Cambridge, MA: MIT Press; 1977: p. 35-57.
  Garvey, William D. *Communication: the essence of science*. Oxford, Eng.: Pergamon Press; 1979: p. 165-173.
5. Gessford, John Evans. *Modern information systems designed for decision support*. Reading, MA: Addison-Wesley; 1980: p. 467-480.
  Sprague, Ralph H., Jr. A framework for the development of decision support systems. *MIS Quarterly*. 4(4): 1-25; 1980 December.
6. Goldstein, Charles M.; Ford, William H. The user-cordial interface. *Online Review*. 2(3): 269-275; 1978.

7. Sharif, Nawaz; Adulbhan, Pakorn. *Systems models for decision making*. Bangkok: Asian Institute of Technology; 1978: p. 325-384.

8. Lancaster, F. Wilfred. *Toward paperless information systems*. New York: Academic Press; 1978: p. 26-27.

9. Salton, Gerald. Toward a dynamic library. *In*: Lancaster, R. Wilfred. *The role of the library in an electronic environment*. Urbana, IL: University of Illinois Graduate School of Library Science; 1979: p. 60-81.

ENGLISH LANGUAGE TRENDS IN GERMAN BASIC SCIENCE JOURNALS: A POTENTIAL COLLECTION TOOL

Tony Stankus
Rashelle Schlessinger
Bernard S. Schlessinger

ABSTRACT. Americans traditionally avoid reading articles in science journals published in foreign languages. By way of response the publishers of some of these journals have progressively increased the proportion of articles in English. That trend is studied here for German basic science journals. Trends tables such as the one reported (for 18 years of 35 journals) can serve librarians in their future decisions about storage and purchase.

Some of the most difficult decisions facing today's librarians relate to the purchase and storage of journals. Methods of studying journals for storage or purchase decisions, such as user questionnaires,[1] tallies of bound volumes left unshelved after use,[2] photocopy requests,[3] circulation records,[4] user publication citation habits,[5] or more generalized citation behavior,[6] have all been reported. To complement these methods in the case of foreign-language journals, this study presents the changing percentage of English-language articles in German basic science journals over time in a table that may serve librarians in future collection development decisions.

Introduction

The background for this study lies in the historical fact that prior to the Second World War, American scientists generally viewed German (and, to a lesser degree, French) research as very important. This was translated into a requirement in undergraduate programs for language training of one (or both) of these languages, and into a requirement in PhD programs for demonstration of reading proficiency in one (or both) of the languages.

After the Second World War, many American scientists gradually accepted the views that:

1. American research was the bellwether research in the scientific community.
2. Most, if not all, substantive research output would eventually be available in the English language.

Tony Stankus (BA, MLS) is Science Librarian at the College of Holy Cross Science Library, Worcester, MA 01610. Rashelle Schlessinger (BA, MLS) is Librarian for the Blind, Department of State Library Services, Providence, RI 02908. Bernard S. Schlessinger (BS, MS, PhD, MLS) is Dean of the Graduate Library School at the University of Rhode Island, Kingston, RI 02881.

3. English was moving toward acceptance as *the* international scientific language.
4. The language of computers was more important to the scientist than reading knowledge of German.

Although these historical perspectives are the interpretations of the authors, their direct manifestations, (1) the elimination of the reading proficiency requirements and substitution of computer language proficiency requirements and (2) the tendency of American library users to ignore foreign language references, can be well-documented.[7-10]

Notwithstanding the changed perceptions of English-language versus foreign-language research noted above, many American researchers still felt a need to use foreign-language materials.[11] This need resulted in two early solutions: (a) provision of accompanying abstracts of foreign-language research and (b) separately requested provision of full translations. Both of these have proved generally unsatisfactory.[12]

Foreign-language journals have recognized that, as the trends noted above developed, their sales to the lucrative American market have decreased. In response, German journals in particular have increasingly allowed or encouraged articles written in English and even "Americanized" or "Internationalized" their titles, formats, and editorial boards.[13] Thus, one can find in the "Instructions for Authors" in *Naturwissenschaften* "English is now the *Lingua Franca* of the sciences and many scientists simply do not read papers published in other languages. Thus, in response to numerous suggestions, and in keeping with the journal's international standing, we herewithal appeal to authors intending to submit short communications to write in English."[14] Similarly there is this note in *Liebig's Annalen der Chemie*[15]—"In an attempt to break down language barriers, the journal has internationalized itself by publishing either German or English papers with summaries in both languages."

Garfield has reported that the "internationalization" movement by German journals has resulted in those journals receiving increasing shares of the citations in their fields.[16] This has obvious implications for increased demand for current subscriptions and for those back years with the better cited English language articles.

The tables below should be of aid in determining: (1) which back years contain sufficient percentages of English-language articles to warrant consideration of purchase, (2) which German journals have moved in the direction of "internationalization" and should be considered (or reconsidered) for inclusion in the collection, and (3) which German journals might be considered for storage only (or for weeding or microform use).

Methodology

German-language journals were chosen for this study, because of the general feeling, both in the literature[17, 18] and of the authors that American scientists consider them the most important foreign-language medium in science.

The German journals with heaviest citations or highest impact listed by Garfield[19] were used for the research provided that:

1. They had a history of publication in Germany in the German language and currently published some papers in English.
2. They were basic-science-oriented. This excluded journals such as those in medicine, pharmacology, medical microbiology, and psychology, etc.

The list of journals used may be found in Table 1.

Each journal issue for the years 1960, 1965, 1970, 1975, 1978 was physically examined by one of the authors, who counted the number of articles in English and determined percentages. Included in the count were full-length articles, communications and letters of at least one page, and extended corrections or replies to criticism of at least one page. Excluded were book reviews, abstracts or oral reports at conferences, obituaries and commemorations, political commentary, and society business.

Results and Discussion

Table 2, which presents the percentage of English-language articles of each journal for the years 1960, 1965, 1970, 1975, and 1978, is interesting in that, of the 35 journals included, 33 show striking increases in percentage of English-language articles from the time they first appear in the table to 1978. Of the two which do not show such a striking increase, one, *Communications of Mathematical Physics*, is already in the 90-100% range on first appearance, while one, *Zeitschrift fuer Anorganische und Allgemeine Chemie* starts out in 1960 at 7.9% and shows only a modest increase to 14.3% in 1975 and 11.2% in 1978. This evidence of internationalization is even more striking if one notes (see Table 3) that 28 of the journals were in the percentage range 0-50 in 1960, while 27 were in the percentage range 75-100 in 1978 (Table 4 lists the 27 journals in the percentage range 75-100). It is of further interest to note that the major shift in philosophy came between 1965 (when 24 journals fell in the 0-50 range) and 1970 (when 22 journals appeared in the 50-100 range). This would seem to have obvious implications for the question of whether to seek back issues before 1970.

Percentage figures show trends, but one must also look at the numbers of articles since that is a possibly more accurate predictor of the demand for a specific journal. Table 5 presents the data for numbers of English-language articles in the 35 journals, 1960-1978. As with the data for percentages in Table 2, these data for numbers show striking increases in English-language articles for each of the 35 journals, with an overall increase in totals from 606 published in English-language articles in 1960 to 7,172 in 1978, a 10.83-fold increase over the 18-year period.

No arguments can be made from these data that include the element of importance to the field of the journals involved. However, the data can be

Table 1. List of Journals Used in the Research

1. Annalen der Physik
2. Anatomy and Embryology
3. Archive for Rational Mechanics and Analysis
4. Archives of Microbiology
5. Astronomy and Astrophysics[a]
6. Berichte der Bunsengesellschaft fuer Physikalische Chemie[b]
7. Cell and Tissue Research[c]
8. Chromosoma
9. Communications of Mathematical Physics[d]
10. Contributions to Mineralogy and Petrology[e]
11. Ctyolobiologie[f]
12. European Journal of Biochemistry[g]
13. Histochemistry[h]
14. Hoppe-Seylers Zeitschrift fuer Physiologische Chemie
15. Inventiones Mathematicae[i]
16. Journal of Comparative Physiology[j]
17. Journal fuer Praktische Chemie
18. Mathematische Annalen
19. Mathematische Zeitschrift
20. Molecular and General Genetics[k]
21. Naturwissenschaften
22. Pflugers Archiv-European Journal of Physiology[l]
23. Physica Status Solidi A+B
24. Planta
25. Synthesis[m]
26. Theoretica Chimica Acta[n]
27. Wilhelm Roux's Archives of Developmental Biology[o]
28. Zeitschrift fuer Anorganische und Allgemeine Chemie
29. Zeitschrift fuer Metallkunde
30. Zeitschrift fuer Naturforschung. Teil A. Physikalische Chemie
31. Zeitschrift fuer Naturforschung. Teil B. Anorganische und Organische Chemie
32. Zeitschrift fuer Naturforschung. Teil C. Biosciences
33. Zeitschrift fuer Pflanzenphysiologie

Table 1 (cont'd)

34. Zeitschrift fuer Physik A and B

35. Zeitschrift fuer Krystallographie

a. established by combination of five journals Annales des Astrophysik, Bulletin of the Astronomical Institute of the Netherlands, Bulletin Astronomie, Journal des Observatorie, and Zeitschrift fuer Astrophysik

b. formerly Zeitschrift fuer Elektochemie

c. formerly Zeitschrift fuer Zellforschung und Mikroskopische Anatomie

d. started in 1965

e. formerly Beitrage zur Mineralogie und Petrologie

f. started in 1969

g. formerly Biochemische Zeitschrift

h. formerly Histochemie

i. started in 1966

j. formerly Zeitschrift fuer Vergleichende Physiologie

k. formerly Zeitschrift fuer Verebungslehre

l. formerly Pfluger's Archiv fuer die Gesamte Physiologie des Menschen

m. started in 1969

n. started in 1962

o. formerly Wilhelm Roux Archiv fuer Entwicklungsmechanik

p. started in 1973

used to provide a picture of those journals that are major volume contributors to English-language publication. In Table 6, it can be seen that five journals contributed 46.4% of all English-language articles published over the 18-year period. Of the five, three are predominantly in Physics, one in Biology, and one in Biochemistry. If more chemical-interest journals are desired, one can move to the second level in Table 6, which includes the nine additional journals that bring the total contribution to 72.5% of all English-language articles published 1960-1978. The distribution of the 14 journals thus included by predominant subject area would be Biology - 6, Chemistry/Biochemistry - 4, Physics - 3, Science - 1. The analysis can be further applied to the other 21 journals that are responsible for the final 26.6% of English-language publication not reflected in Table 6.

Conclusion

This analysis of English-language article publication in German Basic Science journals with high citation or high impact provides a model for developing tools to assist in purchasing or storing foreign language journals.

Table 2. Percentages of English-Language Articles 1960-78

	1960	1965	1970	1975	1978
1. Annalen der Physik	16.2	15.6	19.2	58.8	61.2
2. Anatomy and Embryology	10.0	34.2	36.9	95.6	98.9
3. Archive for Rational Mechanics and Analysis	26.6	88.2	76.1	96.3	94.7
4. Archives of Microbiology	22.0	29.7	72.3	92.3	96.8
5. Astronomy and Astrophysics	38.5	47.7	93.2	95.6	96.4
6. Berichte der Bunsengesellschaft fuer Physikalische Chemie	15.0	4.7	19.9	34.8	79.7
7. Cell and Tissue Research	31.3	54.7	75.4	100.0	100.0
8. Chromosoma	56.3	79.4	91.4	99.1	100.0
9. Communications of Mathematical Physics	----	100.0	98.3	100.0	100.0
10. Contributions to Mineralogy and Petrology	7.1	16.0	80.9	97.5	100.0
11. Cytobiologie	----	----	23.6	76.7	88.6
12. European Journal of Biochemistry	1.5	24.0	93.6	99.6	99.9
13. Histochemistry	43.2	50.5	81.7	93.9	92.6
14. Hoppe-Seylers Zeitschrift fuer Physiologische Chemie	0	0.8	31.8	68.5	91.3
15. Inventiones Mathematicae	----	44.4	71.1	89.6	90.4
16. Journal of Comparative Physiology	21.3	31.1	45.8	70.8	100.0
17. Journal fuer Praktische Chemie	5.6	15.2	16.2	10.9	32.8
18. Mathematische Annalen	39.1	51.8	66.5	66.9	68.9
19. Mathematische Zeitschrift	36.9	50.6	63.2	65.5	66.1
20. Molecular and General Genetics	39.6	39.3	90.1	100.0	99.5
21. Naturwissenschaften	13.3	19.8	37.0	55.2	63.7
22. Pflugers Archiv-European Journal of Physiology	1.6	15.2	71.0	97.1	100.0
23. Physica Status Solidi A+B	11.0	93.0	95.2	99.1	98.4
24. Planta	4.8	24.6	71.2	88.6	100.0

Table 2. (cont'd)

	1960	1965	1970	1975	1978
25. Synthesis	----	----	60.9	78.8	82.5
26. Theoretica Chimica Acta	22.2	52.3	82.5	92.5	94.2
27. Wilhelm Roux's Archives of Developmental Biology	20.4	20.8	52.4	71.7	80.4
28. Zeitschrift fuer Anorganische und Allgemeine Chemie	7.9	5.7	12.6	14.3	11.2
29. Zeitschrift fuer Metallkunde	0.8	1.5	20.6	35.9	39.2
30. Zeitschrift fuer Naturforschung Teil A. Physikalische Chemie	7.9	22.9	40.2	65.4	82.3
31. Zeitschrift fuer Naturforschung Teil B. Anorganische und Organische Chemie	4.8	8.6	23.6	28.2	22.7
32. Zeitschrift fuer Naturforschung Teil C. Biosciences	----	----	----	67.2	76.8
33. Zeitschrift fuer Pflanzenphysiologie	0	11.1	37.4	69.0	75.7
34. Zeitschrift fuer Physik A and B	11.2	19.5	69.3	88.2	99.2
35. Zeitschrift fuer Krystallographie	53.0	71.6	61.0	78.4	80.6

Table 3. Percentage Ranges for English-Language Articles 1960-78

Percentage range	Number of Journals in Range in				
	1960	1965	1970	1975	1978
0-25	21	16	6	2	2
25-50	7	8	6	2	2
50-75	2	4	11	10	4
75-100	0	4	11	2	27

Table 4. The 27 Journals Publishing Better than
75% English-Language Articles in 1978

Anatomy and Embryology

Archive for Rational Mechanics and Analysis

Archives of Microbiology

Astronomy and Astrophysics

Berichte der Bunsengesellschaft fuer Physikalische Chemie

Cell and Tissue Research

Chromosoma

Communications of Mathematical Physics

Contributions to Mineralogy and Petrology

Cytobiologie

European Journal of Biochemistry

Histochemistry

Hoppe-Seylers Zeitschrift fuer Physiologische Chemie

Inventiones Mathematicae

Journal of Comparative Physiology

Molecular and General Genetics

Pflugers Archiv-European Journal of Physiology

Physica Status Solidi A+B

Planta

Synthesis

Theoretica Chimica Acta

Wilhelm Roux's Archives of Developmental Biology

Zeitschrift fuer Naturforschung. Teil A. Physikalische Chemie

Zeitschrift fuer Naturforschung. Teil C. Biosciences

Zeitschrift fuer Pflanzenphysiologie

Zeitschrift fuer Physik A and B

Zeitschrift fuer Krystallographie

Table 5. Numbers of English-Language Articles 1960-78

	1960	1965	1970	1975	1978	Totals
1. Annalen der Physik	6	12	15	30	19	82
2. Anatomy and Embryology	6	13	24	65	90	198
3. Archive for Rational Mechanics and Analysis	41	67	35	78	36	257
4. Archives of Microbiology	20	27	128	168	182	525
5. Astronomy and Astrophysics	82	113	277	499	396	1367
6. Berichte der Bunsengesellschaft fuer Physikalische Chemie	42	11	53	88	200	394
7. Cell and Tissue Research	42	117	307	409	410	1285
8. Chromosoma	18	54	118	110	235	535
9. Communications of Mathematical Physics	----	18	60	116	128	322
10. Contributions to Mineralogy and Petrology	1	4	93	115	92	305
11. Cytobiologie	----	----	13	33	78	124
12. European Journal of Biochemistry	2	49	73	720	726	1570
13. Histochemistry	19	50	125	184	125	503
14. Hoppe-Seylers Zeitschrift fuer Physiologische Chemie	0	1	69	150	136	356
15. Inventiones Mathematicae	----	8	32	43	85	168
16. Journal of Comparative Physiology	13	14	60	138	232	457
17. Journal fuer Praktische Chemie	3	22	24	14	44	107

Table 5 (cont'd)

	1960	1965	1970	1975	1978	Totals
18. Mathematische Annalen	25	71	145	107	124	472
19. Mathematische Zeitschrift	31	78	134	76	109	428
20. Molecular and General Genetics	19	24	128	231	405	807
21. Naturwissenschaften	87	164	125	132	135	643
22. Pflugers Archiv-European Journal of Physiology	4	25	137	134	235	535
23. Physica Status Solidi A+B	9	465	1040	1466	924	3904
24. Planta	6	29	148	171	277	631
25. Synthesis	----	----	53	227	250	530
26. Theoretica Chimica Acta	2	34	132	135	81	384
27. Wilhelm Roux's Archives of Developmental Biology	11	10	22	33	41	117
28. Zeitschrift fuer Anorganische und Allgemeine Chemie	20	20	39	33	35	147
29. Zeitschrift fuer Metallkunde	1	2	32	51	51	137
30. Zeitschrift fuer Naturforschung. Teil A. Physikalische Chemie	15	75	141	191	204	626
31. Zeitschrift fuer Naturforschung. Teil B. Anorganische und Organische Chemie	10	30	90	66	104	300
32. Zeitschrift fuer Naturforschung. Teil C. Biosciences	----	----	----	121	139	260
33. Zeitschrift fuer Pflanzenphysiologie	0	3	55	107	153	318
34. Zeitschrift fuer Physik A and B	36	60	278	351	637	1362
35. Zeitschrift fuer Krystallographie	35	63	47	69	54	266
TOTALS	606	1733	4252	6661	7172	20424

Table 6. Publication of English-Language Articles Rank-Ordered by the Numbers of Such Articles Published

Journal	Numbers of Articles (1960-78)	Total Number of Articles (1960-78)	Percentage of the Total
Physica Status Solidi A+B	3904		
European Journal of Biochemistry	1570		
Astronomy and Astrophysics	1367		
Zeitschrift fuer Physik A and B	1362		
Cell and Tissue Research	1285		
Subtotal for top 5 Journals	9488	20424	46.4
Molecular and General Genetics	807		
Naturwissenschaften	643		
Planta	631		
Zeitschrift fuer Naturforschung. Teil A. Physikalische Chemie	626		
Chromosoma	535		
Pflugers Archiv-European Journal of Physiology	535		
Synthesis	530		
Archives of Microbiology	525		
Histochemistry	503		
Total for top 14 Journals	14823	20424	72.5

REFERENCES

1. Schloman, Barbara Frick; Ahl, Ruth E. Retention periods for journals in a small academic library. *Special Libraries*. 70:377-383; 1979 September.
2. Tibbetts, Pamela. A method for estimating the in-house use of the periodical collection in the University of Minnesota Bio-Medical Library. *Bulletin of the Medical Library Association*. 62:37-48; 1974 January.
3. Basile, Victor A.; Smith, Reginald W. Evolving the 90% pharmaceutical library. *Special Libraries*. 61:88; 1970 February.
4. Kilgour, Frederick G. Use of medical and biological journals in the Yale Medical Library. *Bulletin of the Medical Library Association*. 50:429-443; 1962 July.
5. Chalmers, G. R.; Healey, J. S. Journal citations in masters theses; one measurement of a journal collection. *Journal of the American Society for Information Science*. 24:379-401; 1973 May.
6. Garfield, Eugene. *Journal citation reports; a bibliometric analysis of science journals in the ISI data base*. Philadelphia: ISI; 1979.
7. Schmidt, Jean Mace. Translation of periodical literature in plant pathology. *Special Libraries*. 70:12-17; 1979 January.
8. Gingerich, Owen. Ph.D. language requirement. *Physics Today*. 30:9-10; 1977 November.
9. Sherwood, Bruce A. Universal language requirement. *Physics Today*. 32:9; 1979 July.
10. Leck, Charles F. Foreign languages and biologists today. *Bioscience*. 28:367; 1978 June.
11. Wetzel, Robert G. On foreign languages. *Bioscience*. 28:620; 1978 October.
12. Schmidt, *op. cit.*, p. 13.
13. Schmidt, *op. cit.*, p. 13-14.
14. Instructions for Authors. *Naturwissenschaften*, Inside front cover, each issue.
15. Verlag Chemie International (Prospectus). *Scientific and Technical Journals 1979*, p. 28.

16. Garfield, Eugene. *Essays of an information scientist*. Philadelphia: ISI Press; 1977: p. 470, 473.
17. Schmidt, *op. cit.*, p. 13.
18. Wetzel, *op. cit.*, p. 20.
19. Garfield, *op. cit.*, pp. 471 - 472.

NEW REFERENCE WORKS
IN SCIENCE & TECHNOLOGY

Janice Bain, Editor

[Reviewers for this issue are Carmela Carbone (CC) and Janice Bain (JB).]

ENERGY

Balachandran, Sarojini. *Energy statistics: a guide to information sources*. Detroit: Gale Research Company; 1980. 272 p. $28.00. ISBN 0-8103-1419-3.

This is Volume 1 in the Natural World Information Guide Series. The book is divided into three major sections. The first contains a detailed alphabetical subject/keyword analysis of all recurring statistical data contained in some 40 most used national and international energy serials. Each entry identifies the source that gives the desired information. The second section gives full bibliographical descriptions of the sources analyzed in the first section. The sources are arranged alphabetically by the titles cited in Section I. The third section of the book is an annotated guide to additional sources such as coal, petroleum, electricity, natural gas, nuclear power, and solar power. A separate subject index to Section III is included. A directory of publishers and a personal and corporate author index are also provided. (CC)

ENVIRONMENT

Frick, G. William, ed. *Environmental glossary*. Washington: Government Institutes; 1980. 196 p. $19.50. ISBN 0-86587-080-2.

The 1970s produced many new federal statutes and regulations aimed at protecting the physical environment of the United States. While many regulations created new terminology to implement the statutory and regulatory provisions, many common terms and previously used definitions assumed new meanings. This glossary has attempted to collect these definitions and abbreviations in one location. Key official sources for the definitions have been used, namely, the statutes and the *Code of Federal Regulations*. Generally, each definition is followed by a capital letter, which is a code to designate the source of the definition. The key to the code is provided in the introduction. Uncoded terms are those whose literary warrant is based on unpublished Environmental Protection Agency documents and/or the work of the Government Institutes' research staff. (CC)

METALS

Unterweiser, Paul M., ed. *Worldwide guide to equivalent irons and steels*. Metals Park, Ohio: American Society for Metals; 1979. 575 p. $92.00. ISBN 0-87170-088-3.

This compilation includes the specifications and designations of 34 standards organizations—representing 18 nations—pertaining to steel alloys. The Guide is arranged in seven sections according to major alloy families, beginning with cast irons, followed by cast steels, and concluding with wrought steels. Data entries on individual pages follow a six-column arrangement and give alloy specification number, designation, country of origin, product form, chemical composition, and mechanical properties. Throughout the Guide, all alloys are listed in order of descending carbon content. Other elements listed in the composition follow in fixed order, depending on the class of alloys dealt with. This arrangement generally serves as a mechanical sorter whereby comparable or equivalent alloy compositions are drawn together within close proximity to each other on any given page or series of pages, thus facilitating identification of equivalent alloy compositions. The Guide includes an index by specification number. (CC)

TRANSPORTATION

Reebie Associates, eds. *TRANSGUIDE; a guide to sources of freight transportation information*. Greenwich, Conn.: Reebie Associates; 1980. 381 p. $40.00. ISBN 0-9604776-0-8.

TRANSGUIDE provides a multimodal reference guide to the key international bibliographic sources of general and statistical information on freight transportation. The preface indicates that *TRANSGUIDE* "is designed especially to meet the needs of: industrial transportation management; carrier marketing, operations, and financial management; government and industry association freight transportation planning and research; freight transportation equipment marketing; and transportation industry investment analysis." The reference sources comprising the first of three sections of *TRANSGUIDE* are grouped into eight topical areas: air transportation, commodity classifications, general (all modes), highways and truck transportation, pipelines, railroads and rail transportation, freight traffic flows, and waterways and marine transportation. The entries are annotated. The second section of the guide is an alphabetical listing of vendors and sponsors of the reference sources listed in the first section. Complete order information, including address, telephone number, and price, is included. Each vendor's entry includes a title listing of all works in section one for which he is responsible. The third section is comprised of a subject index and an alphabetical title list of those references listed in the first section. Entries in all three sections utilize an alphanumeric code comprised of an upper case letter denoting topic area, a lower case letter denoting document type, and a numerical indicating the sequence of each entry. (JB)

SCI-TECH ONLINE

Ellen Nagle, Editor

Second National Online Meeting

The Second National Online Meeting, organized by *Online Review*, took place in New York City on March 24-26, 1981. Major sessions covered changing roles in the information industry; library applications of online searching; marketing of online services; the office of the future; management and operation of online services; education and training; measures and evaluations for planning future systems and services; and economic factors. Concurrent with these meetings were product reviews presented by database producers and programs keyed to databases in specific disciplines. There was a large number of exhibitors, both U.S. and foreign, on hand to display wares ranging from computer terminals to new databases. Commercial, governmental, and not-for-profit exhibitors were included in the 60 organizations having booths this year.

The best paper award went to Audrey Clayton for her presentation "Factors affecting future online services." She considered the social, economic, and political factors which will influence the direction, extent, and impact of the technological advances in online services. Published proceedings of the meeting can be ordered from Learned Information, Inc., Box 550, Marlton, NJ 08053 at a cost of $40.

BIOSIS and CAS Report Progress on Taxonomic Indexing Program

BioSciences Information Service (BIOSIS) and Chemical Abstracts Service (CAS) recently reported on the status of a cooperative project initiated in 1972 to establish uniform indexing of the taxonomic nomenclature. Following a CAS report that this type of subject indexing was, after chemical names, the most frequently used indexing entry in the CAS database, BIOSIS proposed to authenticate CAS usage of taxonomic names.

Utilizing computer-readable records from both CAS and BIOSIS databases, a file of more than 80,000 taxonomic names was reviewed by BIOSIS staff and experts in the areas of systematic botany, zoology, and microbiology. Technical advice was also provided by the Academy of Natural Sciences (Philadelphia), Temple University, the University of Pennsylvania, and the Smithsonian Institution.

Other experimental applications are being considered, employing this file as a prototype taxonomic retrieval system. CAS is now employing these names as CA subject headings, resulting in the unification of indexing practices in this area for the two abstracting and indexing services.

Database News

Dow Jones News Database Available through BRS

BRS recently announced the availability of this database, produced by Dow Jones & Company, Inc., publishers of the *Wall Street Journal*, the *Dow Jones News Wire Services*, and *Barrons*, which comprise the database. The database, spanning 90 days of news, had been available since 1974. Dow Jones decided to make it more widely available using BRS software and covering a longer time span. The database will be updated weekly and will cover news stories back to June 1979. Access is by free text searching, as well as by company stock symbol and industry or government codes. Rates are a flat charge of $80 per hour for nonacademic users and $40 per hour for academic users. There is no per citation charge.

PsycINFO Developments

The *Psychological Abstracts* database, now known as *PsycINFO*, is one of 10 databases available on Data-Star, a Radio Suisse operation based in Berne, Switzerland. PsycINFO is now available on five online systems: SDC, BRS, Lockheed, DIDMI (Cologne, Germany), and Data-Star.

PsycINFO is also exploring alternative pricing methods. In a study with a selected group of DIALOG users, a means of keying the royalty revenue to the results of a search, rather than to connect time, is being tested. Users are billed for the citations printed online and offline. PsycINFO welcomes ideas and suggestions regarding equitable pricing structures.

Water Databases Announced by Lockheed

Selected Water Resources Abstracts (SWRA), produced by the U.S. Department of the Interior, is now available on DIALOG. The file is based on materials collected by over 50 water research centers and institutes in the United States, covering water resource economics, ground and surface water hydrology, metropolitan water resources planning and management, and water-related aspects of nuclear radiation and safety. SWRA emphasizes patents, and conference proceedings. The file contains more than 130,000 records from 1968 and will be updated monthly. Available as File 117, the cost is $45 per connect hour and $.15 per full record printed offline. Also available from Lockheed is AQUALINE, File 116. A product of the Water Research Centre, the national center for water research in the United Kingdom, this database gives worldwide coverage to all aspects of water research including waste water and the aquatic environment. Unit records include descriptors assigned from a controlled vocabulary and a descriptive abstract. Coverage is back to 1974 with monthly updates. Charges are $35 per connect hour, $.30 per full record printed offline, and $.25 per full record typed online.

GPO Monthly Catalog Added by BRS

The Government Printing Office *Monthly Catalog* database, going back to July 1976, is now available from BRS. It is a multidisciplinary database of reports, serials, journals, monographs, bibliographies, indexes, and maps, generated by government agencies. Subject coverage includes agriculture, business, law, medicine, engineering, science, social science, the humanities, and public policy and governance. There are more than 100,000 documents in the database, which is updated monthly.

Data Courier Sells Sci-Tech Databases

Loene Trubkin, President of Data Courier, Inc., announced the sale of four of its databases to Cambridge Scientific Abstracts. Effective January 1981, *Pollution Abstracts, Oceanic Abstracts, Conference Papers Index*, and *ISMEC* (Information Science in Mechanical Engineering) are being produced in hard copy as well as in online and tape formats by Cambridge. They promise an orderly transition, with no delay in delivery of update tapes. Data Courier intends to "focus full effort and resources" on expanding ABI/INFORM and to design and develop new databases and services for the international business community. Cambridge Scientific Abstracts, which has published scientific and technical abstracting services for 20 years, can be contacted at (800) 638-8076 with any inquiries or search questions regarding the recently acquired databases.

Search System News

SDC Announces New ORBIT Features

SDC has recently implemented several new search features to enhance its ORBIT search system. Most important are proximity/hierarchical search operators and crossfile searching. Proximity searching enables the system user to specify the hierarchical relationship of terms to one another within the unit record, e.g., one term adjacent to another. This capability will be implemented on the CAS files first and later will be added to other databases. In conjunction with this feature, right-hand, internal, and (on CAS) left-hand truncation can be used. SDC's crossfile features enable searchers to "convert any printable field from relevant records ... into searchable terms" which can then be used to search across multiple files.

Lockheed Lowers SDI Prices

Lockheed reports they have "slashed" SDI prices. Selective Dissemination of Information or current awareness profiles are now available for many of the Lockheed files. Rates vary from $4.95 to $12.95, depending on the database. In addition, the limit of 15 descriptors per profile has been abolished. DIALOG offers discounts up to 40% per profile for 300 or more SDIs stored under one password.

Publications and Search Aids

Getting Acquainted with Online

This free booklet, produced by Data Courier, is intended to acquaint the uninitiated with online searching and to provide information to organizations planning to offer online services. It briefly describes online searching, types of information available online, advantages, costs, and training. Appended to this information are brief listings of computer terminal manufacturers, online vendors, and directories of online databases. Copies of the brochure are available from: Data Courier, Inc., 620 South Fifth Street, Louisville, KY 40202. Phone (800) 626-2823.

Search Aids for Use with DIALOG Databases

Lockheed has compiled this new guide to be used with approximately 100 of the databases it offers. Listed alphabetically by file name, entries include database and users guides, thesauri, authority lists, and other useful search aids.

CHRONOLOG Subscriptions

Lockheed recently announced their new policy of instituting a subscription price to their newsletter for nonactive accounts and nonusers of the Lockheed system. Nonactive accounts are defined as those which have not been used for three consecutive months. Active accounts will continue to get one free copy of *CHRONOLOG*. Subscriptions will be on a calendar year basis, $30.00 in North America and $10.00 elsewhere.

Miscellany

A Note to Our Readers

As we told you in our first issue, the aim of this column is to inform readers about the major developments in online searching relevant to sci-tech libraries. We stated at the time, "Obviously, news items noted here will not be as current to searchers as monthly newsletters or online news messages." No one could foresee, however, the delays in getting our first issues into print. It remains our intention, and the intention of everyone connected with this publication, to provide you with information and opinion about developments in sci-tech online, in as timely a fashion as possible.

For Product Safety Concerns and Information please contact our EU
representative GPSR@taylorandfrancis.com
Taylor & Francis Verlag GmbH, Kaufingerstraße 24, 80331 München, Germany

www.ingramcontent.com/pod-product-compliance
Lightning Source LLC
Chambersburg PA
CBHW052135300426
44116CB00010B/1916